FIELD SERVICE MANAGEMENT

An Integrated Approach to Increasing Customer Satisfaction

THE BUSINESS ONE IRWIN/APICS LIBRARY OF INTEGRATED RESOURCE MANAGEMENT

FIELD SERVICE MANAGEMENT

An Integrated Approach to Increasing Customer Satisfaction

Arthur V. Hill

BUSINESS ONE IRWIN
Homewood, Illinois 60430

Sponsoring editor:	Jeffrey A. Krames
Project editor:	Rita McMullen
Production manager:	Ann Cassady
Compositor:	Alexander Typesetting, Inc.
Typeface:	11/14 Times Roman
Printer:	Book Press, Inc.

Library of Congress Cataloging-in-Publication Data

Hill, Arthur V.
    Field service management : an integrated approach to increasing
customer satisfaction / Arthur V. Hill.
        p.   cm. — (The Business One Irwin/APICS library of integrated
resource management)
    Includes bibliographical references and index.
    ISBN 1-55623-547-X
    1. Customer service.   2. Customer service—Data processing.
    3. Consumer satisfaction. I. Title. II. Series.
HF5415.5.H54   1992
658.8′ 12—dc20   92–6796

This book is dedicated to my wife, Julayne, and our four boys, Christopher, Jonathan, Stephen, and Michael.

FOREWORD

Field Service Management is one book in a series that addresses the most critical issue facing manufacturing companies today: integration—the identification and solution of problems that cross organizational and company boundaries—and, perhaps more importantly, the continuous search for ways to solve these problems faster and more effectively! The genesis for the series is the commitment to integration made by the American Production and Inventory Control Society (APICS). I attended several brainstorming sessions a few years ago in which the primary topic of discussion was, "What jobs will exist in manufacturing companies in the future—not at the very top of the enterprise and not at the bottom, but in between?" The prognostications included:

- The absolute number of jobs will decrease, as will the layers of management. Manufacturing organizations will adopt flatter organizational forms with less emphasis on hierarchy and less distinction between white collars and blue collars.

- Functional "silos" will become obsolete. The classical functions of marketing, manufacturing, engineering, finance, and personnel will be less important in defining work. More people will take on "project" work focused on continuous improvement of one kind or another.

- Fundamental restructuring, meaning much more than financial restructuring, will become a way of life in manufacturing enterprises. The primary focal points will be a new market-driven emphasis on creating value with customers, as well as greatly increased flexibility, a new business-driven attack on global markets which includes new deployment of information technology, and fundamentally new jobs.

- Work will become much more integrated in its orientation. The payoffs will increasingly be made through connections across organizational and company boundaries. Included are customer and vendor partnerships, with an overall focus on improving the value-added chain.

- New measurements that focus on the new strategic directions will be required. Metrics will be developed, similar to the cost of quality metric, that incorporate the most important dimensions of the environment. Similar metrics and semantics will be developed to support the new uses of information technology.

- New "people management" approaches will be developed. Teamwork will be critical to organizational success. Human resource management will become less of a "staff" function and more closely integrated with the basic work.

Many of these prognostications are already a reality. APICS has made the commitment to *leading* the way in all of these change areas. The decision was both courageous and intelligent. There is no future for a professional society not committed to leading-edge education for its members. Based on the Society's past experience with the Certification in Production and Inventory Management (CPIM) program, the natural thrust of APICS was to develop a new certification program focusing on integration. The result, Certification in Integrated Resource Management (CIRM) is a program composed of 13 building block areas which have been combined into four examination modules, as follows:

Customers and products
   Marketing and sales
   Field service
   Product design and development

Manufacturing processes
   Industrial facilities management
   Process design and development
   Manufacturing (production)

Logistics
   Production and inventory control
   Procurement
   Distribution

Support functions
   Total quality management

Human resources
Finance and accounting
Information systems

As can be seen from this topical list, one objective in the CIRM program is to develop educational breadth. Managers increasingly *must* know the underlying basics in each area of the business: who are the people who work there, what are day-to-day *and* strategic problems, what is state-of-the-art practice, what are the expected improvement areas, and what is happening with technology? This basic breadth of knowledge is an absolute prerequisite to understanding the potential linkages and joint improvements.

But it is the linkages, relationships, and integration that are even more important. Each examination devotes approximately 40 percent of the questions to the connections *among* the 13 building block areas. In fact, after a candidate has successfully completed the four examination modules, he or she must take a fifth examination (Integrated Enterprise Management), which focuses solely on the interrelationships among all functional areas of an enterprise.

The CIRM program has been the most exciting activity on which I have worked in a professional organization. Increasingly, manufacturing companies face the alternative of either proactive restructuring to deal with today's competitive realities, or just sliding away—giving up market share and industry leadership. Education must play a key role in making the necessary changes. People working in manufacturing companies need to learn many new things and "unlearn" many old ones.

There were very limited educational materials available to support CIRM. There were textbooks in which basic concepts were covered and bits and pieces which dealt with integration, but there simply was no coordinated set of materials available for this program. That has been the job of the CIRM series authors, and it has been my distinct pleasure as series editor to help develop the ideas and facilitate our joint learning. All of us have learned a great deal, and I am delighted with every book in the series. But the spirit of continuous improvement is built into the CIRM program and into the book series.

Thomas E. Vollmann
Series Editor

PREFACE

This book is designed for professional managers who are either working directly in field service or in areas connected to field service such as sales, manufacturing, logistics, or engineering. The book clearly communicates important management principles than can empower a field service organization to achieve breakthrough levels in both customer satisfaction and productivity. The theme of the book is that field service organizations can achieve these performance breakthroughs by better managing the interfaces with other areas such as sales, manufacturing, logistics, and engineering. The result of this integrated approach to managing field service is improved customer satisfaction and higher productivity—which results in higher profitability.

Many people made significant contributions to this book. I want to give particular recognition to the following people (in alphabetical order):

Jim Bahr, 3M Company

Mark Bittenbender, Digital Equipment Corporation

Richard Bredehoft, Detector Electronics

Mike Burns, Service Systems International

Gegi Carlson, TCF Bank Savings

Walt Coleman, Whirlpool

Ilene DeJong, Advances System Technologies, Inc.

Phil Dismuke, Norstan Communications, Inc.

Dale Findell, TRW Inc.

Mike Gibson, 3M Company

Jim Hall, 3M Company

Dyan Haugen, University of Minnesota

Craig Kalscheur, Norstan Communications

Bob McGuire, Digital Equipment Corporation

Larry Miller, Service Systems International

Dan Minnix, 3M Company

Dave Naumann, University of Minnesota

Gary Ragatz, Michigan State University

Ash Rao, Babson College

Fran Romo, TRW, Inc.

Steve Rosenthal, Boston University

Barb Schmit, National Computer Systems

Rich Scorza, Norstan Communications, Inc.

Gary Scudder, Vanderbilt University

Pete Stanaitis, 3M Company

Don Uggla, 3M Company

Fred Van Bennekom, Boston University

Jim Van Til, Whirlpool

Gene Vietor, Control Data Corporation

Tom Vollmann, IMD

Paul Weinberg, The DataGroup

I firmly believe in continuous improvement. Your feedback on this book is greatly appreciated. Please send your suggestions to me so that I can share them with others in the next edition of the book. My address is:

Professor Arthur V. Hill
Curtis L. Carlson School of Management
271 19th Avenue South
University of Minnesota
Minneapolis, Minnesota 55455

Phone: 612-624-4015
Fax: 612-626-1316
Internet: AHILL@CSOM.UMN.EDU

CONTENTS

CHAPTER 1

INTRODUCTION TO FIELD SERVICE MANAGEMENT

A major manufacturer of personal computers is currently running an advertisement that refers to its competitors with the following statement: "Notebook computers are incredibly lightweight—unfortunately, so is most of their own service and support." They go on to claim that their own lightweight computer is "heavy on service and support." This advertisement and many others like it testify to the significance of service and support in many markets today.

This book is about managing field service repair for equipment such as:

- Computers and peripherals.
- Communication systems.
- Office equipment (copy machines, facsimile machines, etc.).
- Medical equipment.
- Heating and cooling equipment.
- Home appliances.
- Factory equipment (robots, NC machines, etc.).

The goal of this book is improvement of field service operations for increased customer satisfaction and field service productivity. It is designed to be of immediate help to managers in a wide variety of field service areas as well as to those outside who desire a better understanding of field service management issues. Managers in companies that maintain their own equipment will also find these concepts valuable.

Many organizations can achieve breakthrough levels of performance by better managing the interfaces between field service and other areas such as sales, manufacturing, logistics, and engineering. An integrated approach to managing field service results in greater product utility and overall customer satisfaction.

The Field Service Business

Field service organizations employ technicians (field service engineers, field engineers, customer service representatives, etc.) who install machines, perform preventive or emergency maintenance in the field, and provide on-site training. Many manufacturers employ field service organizations that provide field service under warranty coverage bundled with the purchase price. Most service providers offer service agreements that provide for service after the warranty has expired and also support "time and materials" charges, where the customer pays for actual labor and/or materials required for the repair.

Field service is a relatively new profession. By most accounts, field service, as we know it today, did not exist before World War II. Today, U.S. companies such as IBM and Xerox employ many thousands of technicians in the field. At least 500,000 technicians are employed in the United States, and by some accounts, this number is increasing (Fowler, 1990).

Field service organizations are very diverse. Large organizations employ thousands of technicians, whereas the local appliance store may use only one. Some field service organizations deal with high-technology equipment such as medical imagers, while others may specialize in low-technology equipment such as toilets. Equipment ranges in size from the extremely large cooling tower recently installed at the world's largest shopping center to the knob on the desktop copy machine in a business office. This book will discuss the entire range of field service organizations. The book will use the term *machine* while recognizing that in many environments a more appropriate term would be *system*. The term *machine* is used generically throughout the book.

If a company repairs the equipment it manufactures and/or distributes itself, it is called "first-party" service. If the organization repairs its own equipment, it is called "second-party" service. These organizations are also called "self-maintainers." (The terms *first-party* and *second-party* are not widely used in the industry.) If the organization repairs equipment from other vendors, it is called "third-party" service. Third-party service (TPS) companies are often either large national companies that support many different products or smaller regional companies focusing on only a few products. If a company provides service such as depot repair to second- or third-party service providers, it is sometimes called "fourth-party" service. The focus of this book will be on first-party and third-party service; however, many of these concepts are also useful for self-maintainers and fourth-party service organizations.

Field service organizations generally service equipment either on-site, or the customer brings the machine to a "depot" for repair. A combination of the two is also common.

Equipment maintenance is becoming more important in modern societies as complex electronic equipment has become a critical part of the infrastructure of nearly all hospitals, factories, buildings, offices, and homes. In the past many companies and individuals repaired their own equipment, but this is no longer feasible in many cases due to the complexity of the equipment. Electronic repair used to involve simply testing a circuit. Today, it involves complex networks of integrated circuits and software. New technology has many potential hiding places for "bugs" and is, therefore, much harder to diagnose and repair in the field.

Although modern electronic equipment is becoming more complex, the cost of many computer-based technologies has declined. Since field service organizations often base the price of the service agreement on the equipment purchase (or lease) price, these organizations are now squeezed by declining profit margins. Other factors contributing to reduced profit margins include:

- Declining hardware unit revenues.
- Increasing product complexity.
- Expanding customer expectations.
- Intensifying competition.

Some service organizations continue to be profitable due to increases in unit sales, product reliability, and/or breadth of services; however, many others are beginning to lose substantial amounts of money in this new, more difficult environment.

When repair is done at the customer site (field service repair), the service organization employs dispatchers who receive service calls from customers requesting on-site repairs. After determining by phone consultation that an on-site repair cannot be avoided, the service call is assigned to an available technician or put into a queue of calls until a technician becomes available. Some companies have an account representative relationship between the technician and the customer and immediately assign the call to the technician responsible for that machine. When a technician calls the dispatcher to request the next service call, the dispatcher selects a call from the queue according to some dispatching rule and assigns the service call to the technician. The technician then calls the customer and, if needed, proceeds to the customer's site, diagnoses the problem, and attempts to repair the machine. If the required parts are not available, the parts are ordered and the machine remains "down" until the part arrives and the machine is repaired on a second visit to the customer site.

Figure 1–1 describes the typical emergency maintenance service call. As the figure indicates, response time includes both queue time and travel time but not repair time. For most field service repair systems, queue time is by far the longest portion of the response time for the call. Queue time is a function of technician utilization, which is based on the arrival rate of calls, travel time, machine repair time, and the dispatching/scheduling rules that are applied to sequence and schedule technicians. Machine downtime can be much longer than the normal service cycle if the necessary parts are not immediately available.

FIGURE 1–1
Time Line for a Typical Emergency Maintenance Call

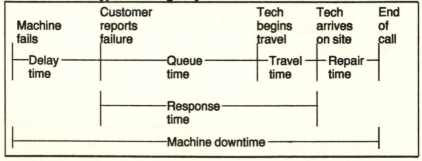

Many service providers define service quality primarily in terms of average response time. However, customers often define service quality in terms of how long the machine is down. Machine downtime is affected by the response time for the technician to arrive on-site, the repair time, and the availability of any required parts. This subject will be explored in much more detail in other chapters.

The "delay time" at the beginning of the service cycle is caused by the end-user not immediately identifying the problem or by cumbersome accounting/clerical procedures that may be required before a service request is communicated to the service provider. Some sophisticated machines now have self-diagnosis and reporting features that make it possible for the machine to automatically detect a problem and phone the service provider (via modem) to report the problem.

HIERARCHY OF DECISIONS FOR FIELD SERVICE MANAGEMENT

Field service management involves a hierarchy of decisions regarding business strategy, field service system design, and operating policies. Each of these is discussed below.

Business Strategy

The business strategy should define how the organization includes field service in the bundle of goods and services that the organization offers as a product to the marketplace. Field service is an important product attribute in many industries. Evidence of this is found in numerous professional magazines, such as *Business Week,* which regularly carry advertisements for companies claiming to have excellent field service. Forgetting to explicitly consider field service in the business/marketing strategy can lead to an incoherent and ineffective market position. On the other hand, companies such as IBM, Xerox, and Tennant have found that explicitly including field service in their business strategies has contributed substantially to their success. A good business strategy requires decisions regarding how field service is used in defining its market niche, advertising, and contractual relationships with customers. Excellent field service can allow an organization to occupy a superior service market niche and, therefore, gain competitive advantage. Clearly, warranties, service agreements, service guarantees, and service performance measures must support the overall organization's business strategy. These and other issues are explored in more detail in the following chapters.

Field Service System Design

Field service system design involves deciding how many technicians to have, what areas these technicians should cover, how to position service parts inventories, and several other tactical issues. The design of the field service system determines many of the controllable field service costs and, to a large degree, the service levels that will be provided to the customers given the field service strategy. These and other related issues are explored in the chapters on performance measurement, service call management, and service parts inventory management.

Operating Policies

Operating policies guide the day-to-day operating decisions. Policies must be defined regarding rules for replenishing inventory, dispatching technicians, processing service calls, supplying backup equipment, and so forth. These policies also have significant impact on the performance of the field service system. Often these operational details make the difference between the good and the excellent field service organization.

This book will address all three levels of decisions in the field service business. Many of the operational issues are available in end-of-chapter appendixes.

FIELD SERVICE OBJECTIVES

The goals of a field service organization include the following:

- *Maximize uptime:* the operational and functional view of the service provider-customer relationship.
- *Exceed customer expectations:* the perceptual view of the service provider-customer relationship.

- *Achieve financial objectives:* the financial view of the service provider-customer relationship.

Each of these is discussed below.

Maximize Uptime

Customers purchase or lease equipment in order to achieve their organizational objectives. If the customer's system is not fully operational, the customer's objectives are blocked and an opportunity cost is incurred. The service organization should view itself as a partner with the customer and should attempt to minimize the customer's opportunity cost for machine downtime. (Note: Machine downtime + Machine uptime = Total hours of operation.)

Many experienced field service managers argue that response time is more important than machine uptime. Clearly, it is true that response time is important to end-users because response time is usually the largest segment of machine downtime and because response time has a major impact on the end-user's perception of the service. However, we can separate the operational and perceptual issues. Machine uptime is the dominant issue with respect to customer operations. The customer incurs an opportunity cost for the lost use of the equipment during the time that the machine is not operational. Response time is just one segment of this time. As discussed in the next section, response time is one of many issues that affect customer satisfaction.

Exceed Customer Expectations

Service quality can be defined in a pseudomathematical way as:

$$
\begin{aligned}
\text{Service quality} &= \text{Satisfaction with service delivery} \\
&= \text{Perceived service delivery} - \text{Expected service delivery} \\
&= P - E
\end{aligned}
$$

When the customer perceives that the service actually delivered (P) exceeds the expected service (E), the customer is satisfied and judges it to be a quality service. However, when customer expectations are not satisfied, the service is judged to be of poor quality.

Response times are an important issue for many end-users. If the service agreement promises a 3-hour response time and the technician has a 13-hour response time, the customer will not be satisfied. Clearly, the service provider must manage *both* the service delivery and the customer's expectations to avoid negative values for P − E. Expectations can be managed simply by the technician keeping the customer informed when plans need to be changed. These issues will be discussed further in the chapter on service quality. The result of exceeding customer expectations is that customers will be satisfied and will continue to purchase hardware, service agreements, service parts, supplies, software, training, and other related products.

Achieve Financial Objectives

The basic components of the financial picture of a service organization include:

- Revenues from service agreements, service parts, supplies, billable labor, other services (training, installation, etc.).
- Costs for labor (technicians, dispatchers, and other), training, parts, warehouses, vehicles, information systems, communications systems, management, offices, and other overhead. (Overhead often makes up over 50 percent of the total cost.)

A field service organization can be operated as a "cost center" or a "profit center." The explicit goal of the cost center approach is that the service organization will maximize customer satisfaction with respect to warranty service, response times, machine uptime, machine downtime, and so on, subject to the budget constraint. This is a common arrangement for many field service organizations that are a division of a manufacturing company.

The goal of the profit center approach is to find the right blend of services that generates more revenues than costs. Field service directly generates revenues such as mentioned above. Field service also generates indirect revenues by influencing hardware sales and leases and sales of other complementary products (e.g., software). Unfortunately, these rarely can be directly assigned to field service as revenues. A good field service organization can generate a stream of revenues long after a product is no longer being manufactured and, thus, help to smooth and extend the revenue stream for a manufacturing organization. This annuitylike cash flow can make a significant contribution to the company's financial performance.

Most service organizations pursue some form of profit center approach. However, it is difficult to pursue the profit center approach when the relationships between service levels, profits, and revenues are not clear. Warranty repair, for example, is not profitable for the service organization but is absolutely necessary for hardware sales.

The cost center approach is not much easier. It is important to maintain tight financial controls so that field service does not become a "black hole" that consumes undue resources. The budget constraint should be guided by a coherent field service strategy, and costs should be carefully managed so that they are kept in line with revenues.

No matter how field service is treated in terms of financial controls, it is clear that field service performance has a major impact on customer perceptions, revenues, and costs. For many companies, field service is one of the last untapped opportunities for competitive advantage.

OVERVIEW OF THE BOOK

The remainder of this book is structured as follows:

Chapter 2. Field Service Strategy: Managing the Field Service Business for Competitive Advantage. This chapter discusses the strategic impact of field service and outlines a process for developing a field service strategy.

Chapter 3. Performance Measurement for Field Service: Managing by the Numbers. This chapter overviews a number of performance measurement issues for field service systems. Many field service organizations have "shot themselves in the foot" by not understanding and applying these concepts correctly.

Chapter 4. Service Quality Management: Managing Customer Satisfaction. Service quality is widely misunderstood. This chapter presents a simple but profound framework for understanding and measuring service quality for a field service organization. Customer surveys and benchmarking concepts are presented in this chapter as the basic external measurements needed to form the basis for service quality management.

Chapter 5. Service Call Management: Managing the Customer Interface.   Service calls are the basic transactions of a field service business. Managing the service call is managing the customer. This chapter presents issues such as service call data entry, assignment, escalation, clearing, cycle time reduction, dispatcher staffing, centralization of dispatching, technical assistance center, and software support/helpdesk management.

Chapter 6. Service Parts Inventory Management: Managing the Inventory Investment.   This chapter gives extensive analysis on how to manage service parts and repairable inventories. Much of the cost and revenue for field service is related to the parts side of the business. Extensive appendixes are included for those interested in the operational details of service parts management.

Chapter 7. Service Management Information Systems: Managing the Field Service Information Resource.   This chapter describes the information systems that are needed to manage a field service business.

Chapter 8. Interfunctional Connections: Managing the Integrated Organization.   This chapter investigates the relationships between field service, sales/marketing, design engineering, manufacturing, and information systems.

Chapter 9. Advanced Technologies for Field Service Management: Managing Technology for Competitive Advantage.   This chapter discusses several emerging technologies and predicts how they will impact field service management in the future.

Case studies are placed at the end of many chapters. These case studies are designed to illustrate the points presented in the chapters and will help the reader integrate and apply the principles communicated in the book. The cases also illustrate the wide variety of field service organizations and field service activities.

Posted in an office copy room:
COPY MACHINE TEMPORARILY -N-O-T- OUT OF ORDER

Source: *Readers Digest,* September 1991.

CASE STUDY

Whirlpool Minneapolis Consumer Services Branch

COMPANY BACKGROUND

Whirlpool Corporation, a $6.6 billion global corporation headquartered in Benton Harbor, Michigan, is a leading manufacturer of major home appliances. Whirlpool's products include a large variety of home appliances including refrigerators, dishwashers, freezers, washers and dryers, trash compactors, gas and electric ranges, and microwave ovens. Whirlpool's major brands are Whirlpool, KitchenAid, Roper, and several brands outside the United States. Major competitors include General Electric, Frigidaire, and Maytag.

Whirlpool has historically used RCA and a network of local dealers to provide service. However, in recent years, Whirlpool has made the strategic decision to provide its own service in many major metropolitan areas. In the words of Jim Van Til, the Minneapolis branch manager, this strategic move has allowed Whirlpool to begin to "capture brand loyalty by capturing the service experience."

MINNEAPOLIS CONSUMER SERVICES BRANCH

Whirlpool has decentralized call taking, dispatching, and technician management. The Minneapolis branch was opened in 1990 and serves the Minneapolis/St. Paul metropolitan area. The branch staff includes:

- one manager.
- eight technicians.
- two call takers who take calls from customers.
- one dispatcher who deals primarily with technicians and helps with accounting.
- one parts coordinator.
- one branch accountant.

SERVICE CALL MANAGEMENT

When a call is received, the call coordinator enters information on a computer terminal connected to a host computer in Indiana. Consumer file information is found based on the consumer's phone number. Parts orders are directed to the parts coordinator. Product-use questions are directed to the Consumer Assistance Center (CAC) in either Benton Harbor, Michigan, or Knoxville, Tennessee. The CAC uses sophisticated systems to provide use and care information and to assist consumers in fixing their appliances. These systems can use artificial intelligence and customer databases to assist the consumer.

In the Minneapolis branch, technician schedules are displayed on a board on the wall for the next six days. When a service call requires an on-site visit, the call coordinator finds an unfilled half-day (A.M. or P.M.) slot in the schedule of a technician who works in the area, and promises the time to the consumer. (ZIP codes are used to define the areas and the consumer locations.) Response time is usually within one or two days.

About one-half of the technicians check into the Minneapolis branch every day to pick up parts and to get their schedules for the next day. The other half receive their parts and their work orders by a delivery service that picks up the parts and work orders from the Minneapolis branch at 4:30 P.M. each day and delivers them directly to the technician's van sometime during the evening or night (sometimes as late as 2 A.M.) so that the technician has the parts and work orders available for the next morning.

All technicians have cellular phones and are required to call the consumers just before beginning travel to a consumer's site. The cellular phones are judged to help productivity and customer satisfaction but are fairly expensive.

Many service calls are on service agreements. Many others are cash calls. Cash calls have a trip charge and a labor charge based on standard costs. Service calls for sealed systems (e.g., compressors for cooling and refrigeration systems) are charged on the basis of time.

Whirlpool does not have a primary technician (account representative) assigned to each consumer. Instead, Whirlpool technicians are assigned overlapping territories. Service calls are assigned to the technicians who are available and will be working in the vicinity of the consumer. This makes sense for Whirlpool because of the large number of consumers.

Technician schedules are loaded to finite capacity for each half-day period. The load for any half-day period is a function of the types of service calls and the expected travel times.

The manager adds more technicians to the work force when overtime costs and response times become unacceptably high. This process is complicated by the fact that the business tends to be seasonal, with slower business in the winter. The winter slowdown is probably due to the fact that air conditioning and refrigeration equipment are stressed more in the summer months.

SERVICE PARTS

Technician vehicles are restocked on a one-for-one basis. At the start of each business day, a technician provides the parts coordinator with a list of parts that were used the previous day. (On an emergency basis, technicians can call for expedited parts delivery.) The parts coordinator then replenishes those parts for the technician's "truck stock." Technicians are responsible for stocking their own vans. They consider branch information on parts usage rates, service incidence rates, and new model information to tailor their truck inventories to their service needs. Service technicians also order parts through the parts coordinator.

PERFORMANCE MEASUREMENT

Performance measurement for technicians is based on three variables:

Productivity. Productivity is measured by the average number of completed calls per day. Most technicians are servicing between 8 and 10 calls per day. Of these, 92 to 94 percent are fully completed without need for any additional repair or additional nonstock parts.

Quality. Whirlpool's corporate office administers a phone survey of 13 consumers per technician each month. Due to the nature of the consumers, the phone surveys are usually done in the afternoons and evenings. The target is for 95 percent of all consumers to be either satisfied or very satisfied with the service experience.

Sales. Sales are measured on the basis of revenues from labor, parts, accessory sales, and service contracts.

CHALLENGES

One of the biggest challenges is meeting (and exceeding) consumer scheduling expectations. This is particularly difficult now that many families have two wage earners. The Minneapolis branch is trying to develop creative ways to meet these needs. An effort is also underway to attempt to increase the percentage of service calls that are completed on the first call. The primary issue here is having the parts that are needed by the consumer.

KEY POINTS

Even though the Whirlpool Minneapolis branch is small, the strategic nature of field service is clear. If Whirlpool wants to capture consumer loyalty, it must capture the "service experience."

The dispatching and scheduling procedures at Whirlpool are very different from those in many other field service environments. This difference is justifiable, given the industry practice and the number of different consumers that are serviced. It would not be reasonable for Whirlpool to have account representatives for its many consumers.

Lastly, technicians define the target levels in their own vehicles, and the system replenishes each item used the previous day. This one-for-one replenishment policy appears to be a very simple and effective way to manage the vehicle inventories.

ACKNOWLEDGEMENTS

The author thanks Mr. Jim Van Til, branch manager for the Whirlpool Minneapolis Consumer Services Branch, for his help in preparing this case.

CHAPTER 2

FIELD SERVICE STRATEGY: MANAGING THE FIELD SERVICE BUSINESS FOR COMPETITIVE ADVANTAGE

INTRODUCTION

Markets are becoming more sophisticated. Having the lowest initial cost is less likely to guarantee a sale. Customers now consider the total cost of a purchase—including the initial cost, the cost of service, and the cost of downtime over the life of the product. Chase and Garvin (1989) argue persuasively that the service side of many products is the next major competitive battleground.

Field service, therefore, plays an important role in the business strategy for many firms. This is particularly true for many manufacturing and value-added retailers that often win or lose orders on the basis of service. Field service management can have an impact on:

Advertising

Many business and professional magazines are loaded with advertisements that claim first class service for their products. These and many other advertisements attest to the fact that field service can play an important role in an advertising strategy. Of course, it is important that the advertisements do not subtlely communicate that the product *needs* an exceptional amount of service. The messages should include ideas such as "our products are so good, we guarantee them" or "we are committed to being your partners and we will come to your site to fix your equipment if you ever have a problem."

Market Position

The importance of field service goes far beyond just advertising. Field service performance impacts the service provider's reputation which in turn impacts sales of new equipment, facilitating products (e.g., software, supplies), service agreements, and so forth. A reputation for good field service enhances customer perceptions for the service provider's entire line of products.

Field service can give the service organization the ability to compete successfully in highly profitable market niches. Very often, the time-sensitive customer is one who relies heavily on the equipment for success and is, therefore, willing to pay more for the equipment, to buy more equipment, and to update the equipment sooner. For example, companies A and B both purchase a special kind of copy machine. Company B seldom uses the machine, is not very concerned about service, and will probably never buy another machine. However, the copy machine is the heart of the business for Company A. Clearly, Company A needs to have a service agreement that will protect it from downtime. The time-sensitive customer (Company A) is less price-sensitive, will buy more facilitating products (e.g., paper, supplies), and is more likely to buy additional equipment. Competing on field service, rather than price, is a better strategy for many organizations because it stratifies the market. The time-sensitive, high-margin, loyal, high-volume customers gravitate to the best service providers. (In their excellent book, *Competing Against Time*, Stalk and Hout support the above points with respect to response times.)

Customer Perception of Risk

Good warranties, service agreements, and a competent field service organization to support these adds value to the customer as a type of "insurance policy" against the risk of unacceptable downtime. Customers are often willing to pay a premium in order to have the assurance that large opportunity costs will not be incurred.

Customer Contact

An often-overlooked fact is that field service people usually have more contact with the customer than any other company representative, including the sales representatives. If the service organization has consistently done a good job over the life of the product, the technician and customer both view themselves as partners, customer loyalty is won, and the sales representative's job is simplified to that of explaining the new product lines and taking the next order. Companies must begin to think about this relationship from a strategic viewpoint.

Profitability

Field service financial performance also has a direct impact on company profitability. Revenues from service agreements and service parts alone are often very significant. Warranty repair, technician labor, and inventory carrying costs are also very significant and can have a major impact on profitability.

STRATEGY FORMULATION

Clearly, field service has important strategic implications. Companies can use field service to differentiate their products from the competition. However, the company must define a consistent strategy with respect to field service and this strategy must be communicated and accepted companywide so that the long-term strategic benefits can be realized. This strategy affects design engineering, manufacturing, sales, and many other areas of the business. This chapter presents the issues that all field service organizations should consider as they seek to formulate a coherent and consistent field service strategy. These decisions include:

Market Position.   Given our assessment of our environment and competition, how should the product be positioned in the market? Should we compete on the basis of price, product quality, field service, or other services? How should we structure our service agreements? Should we offer service guarantees?

Service Guarantees   Should we guarantee our field service with respect to response times, uptimes, etc? What penalty should be built into this service guarantee?

Customer Interface   How should we manage our relationship to the customer? Should we have customers bring their machines to our depot? Should we have technicians establish an account representative relationship with our customers?

Third-Party Service Providers   Should we provide the service with our own technicians or rely on a third-party service provider? Should we form an alliance with another firm to provide service?

Organizational Reporting Relationship   Where does the field service organization report within the overall organizational structure?

Complementary Products   What products and services should we offer through our field service organization so that we can "own" the customer?

Each of these strategic decisions is discussed below.

Market Position

Formulating a field service strategy should begin with an assessment of many environmental issues. These issues include:

- Machine population: How many machines are in the area? How many are expected to be placed in the foreseeable future?
- Machine density (machine population/area): This is the machine population divided by the area covered. Although this is not often measured quantitatively, the concept is a useful one. The ideal environment has high machine density, low travel times, and short response times. It is very difficult for a service organization to be profitable in a low-density service area. A low-density area will tend to have high travel times and long response times. In a low-density area, technicians do not see very many failures and tend to have trouble maintaining proficiency which results in problems of completing service calls on the first visit. Service parts inventories are kept low which often results in problems with completing service calls during the first site-visit. The cost per repair is higher because of travel times, lower technician utilization, and higher parts transportation costs. Cus-

tomer perception of the service is generally poor because of poor response time and poor first call effectiveness.

- Competition: In areas with more competitors, the service provider may have to deliver better service. Analysis of the competition should consider pricing, service contracts, response times, customer satisfaction, etc. Expectations are often set by the competition.
- Industry practice: Some industries have a widely accepted industry practice that constrains strategic alternatives.
- Product technology: Product technology is a part of the field service strategy in many ways. The field service strategy should consider the product life, the mean time between failure (MTBF), mean time to repair (MTTR), mean time to diagnose (MTTD), design for serviceability, internal diagnostics, etc. Product design determines a very large percentage of the overall costs and has a major influence on service strategies.
- Opportunity cost of customer downtime: Critical applications, such as hospital equipment, require better response times than do noncritical applications.

After a thorough environmental assessment has been done on the above variables, the marketing management and field service management should consider the market position of the company's products with respect to field service. For example, Company X, a rapidly growing manufacturer and value-added retailer of personal computers, has a good limited warranty (one year full parts and labor, 30-day money-back guarantee, toll-free 24-hour/7-day-per-week telephone support) but does not bundle on-site service as a part of its warranty agreement. Company X will provide on-site service, but it does not come with the warranty. X's service is primarily through the technician support line and depot repair and has been given high ratings in the popular computer magazines. In contrast, Company Y has the same basic limited warranty, but does provide on-site service (through a third-party service) if the technician support people cannot solve the problem over the telephone. Y's service has also been rated highly. Both X and Y are using service as a competitive weapon, but they have implemented fairly different service strategies with regard to on-site service.

The marketing strategy can also be regional in nature. As mentioned above, density is a major determinant of profitability. It is far better to target a city than it is to market the product broadly. This may be achieved by means of pricing (zone charges, multisystem discounts, etc.) and/or advertising. It makes sense in some situations to sell system redundancy with equipment that is not in a primary service zone. Mr. Gene Vietor, a former Control Data Corporation executive, states that, "The criticality of developing and executing a density-driven marketing plan cannot be overemphasized." No matter what strategy is pursued with respect to the machine density issue, it is important to manage customer expectations regarding response time and downtime.

Service Guarantees

Service guarantees are becoming very popular in a number of service industries as a way to achieve a unique market position. Service guarantees can often endow a service organization with breakthrough capabilities that allow it to dominate a market. Most people assume that the only benefits of a service guarantee are primarily marketing related; however, service guarantees benefit operations just as much (or more) than marketing. Hart (1988) describes many useful examples of how service guarantees have allowed service organizations to achieve breakthrough performance.

The essence of this concept is that a service guarantee clearly defines the bundle of goods and services that is offered to the customer and what the service provider must do to make good on a broken promise. In the field service business, these guarantees are often expressed in terms of a guaranteed uptime or a phone response time from a technician. Service guarantees have five major benefits.

1. *A service guarantee forces you to focus on customers.* Many field service organizations measure themselves against internal standards that have little relationship to how the customer perceives the service. For example, a company may measure mean response time, but the customer may be more concerned about the worst case response time. A service guarantee causes the service provider to satisfy a predefined standard that is known to the customer. This customer focus has benefit for educating new employees and for system design.

2. *A guarantee sets clear standards*. Field service managers and technicians nearly always want to satisfy customers. However, the standards are often very loosely defined. A service guarantee (such as a three-hour response time or free service for one month) sets a very clear standard for both the service provider and the customer.

3. *A guarantee generates feedback*. All managers agree that it is of great value to get regular customer feedback to improve the process, but few customers ever complain on their own initiative. The service agreement is a useful way of encouraging negative feedback that can be used to feed the continuous improvement process.

4. *A guarantee forces you to understand why you failed*. A subtle but very significant aspect of a service guarantee is that it stresses the organization when a service failure occurs. This stress can be very positive in terms of directing everyone's attention toward process improvement. The information about the service failure becomes immediate and specific feedback that can be used for self-improvement.

All organizations are subject to crusades—including cost-reduction crusades. A good service guarantee will make it more difficult for a well-intended, cost-cutting crusade to cut right into customer service. In the absence of a service guarantee, it may take a long time for the service provider to discover that service quality has been forgotten.

5. *A guarantee has significant marketing advantages*. This is the most obvious (but not necessarily most important) aspect of a service guarantee. The service guarantee is often very attractive to the risk-averse customer who is concerned about machine downtime. By including a service guarantee, the service provider is selling an "insurance" policy to the customer. The marketing leverage of a service guarantee is related to service guarantees that are already on the market. If a company is the first to market with a service guarantee, it may gain a significant marketing advantage over the competition and may allow the service provider to quickly get down the service quality learning curve. However, if the service provider is not the first to market with a service guarantee, the company may be at a serious disadvantage because the competition may have already attracted the risk-averse market segment and may be well down the learning curve on satisfying the guarantee. Companies not first to market may be left with the price-sensitive, low-margin customers who do not need the service very much.

Customer Interface

At a strategic level, service providers have a number of alternatives for relating to their customers including:

- On-site repair (technicians travel to the customer site).
- Depot repair (customers carry machines to the service provider for repair).
- Return to manufacturing (customers send machines to be repaired).

On-site repair is more common for very expensive and/or large machines. This is particularly true for repair of integrated systems that need to be tested as a system rather than as independent components. Less expensive, smaller machines and machines that need special repair equipment (e.g., computer monitors) are often repaired at a central repair depot. Many customers (e.g., retailers) want on-site service even for inexpensive, smaller machines simply because of the cost of disconnecting and transporting the machine to the depot. The cost of depot repair is generally around 65 percent of the cost of field service repair.

Many service companies find it more economical for technicians to travel from call to call and not return to a home office. However, if the demand rate is low, depot work is available, or parts need to be picked up, it might be economical to have the technicians return to a home base after most calls. For example, Texas Instruments makes very good use of its technicians with a depot repair operation that maintains a steady workload.

Some companies, such as Whirlpool and Digital Equipment Corporation (DEC), avoid having a technician make an unnecessary trip to a home office by using local delivery services (dispatch services) that pick up and deliver parts in large metropolitan areas. The cost for these services is often less than that of a technician. Whirlpool has parts for the next day's work delivered at night to the technician's van at the technician's residence.

Some service organizations are designed so that some or all technicians have an account representative relationship with their customers. The advantages of having this type of relationship are substantial.

The customers develop a relationship with "their tech." This kind of relationship can facilitate quick communications and can result in increased sales of service agreements, hardware, and supplies.

The problem with the account representative relationship is that it constrains the dispatchers to assign only the one account representative (or a backup) to a particular call. If the account representative is busy, the response time on the call may suffer while another qualified technician may be sitting idle. A compromise solution here is to have a primary, secondary, and even a tertiary technician assigned to each account. The first of these technicians that is available is assigned to the call. At DEC, the primary account representative will nearly always make the initial phone contact with the customer; the service call will then be handed off to another technician if necessary.

For some very expensive machines (e.g., large mainframes), the account representative may reside in the customer's building. These are sometimes called resident technicians.

The account representative concept makes sense in situations where:

- The customer/technician relationship is very important. This is true where the need for empathy and assurance is high.
- The number of customers is not very large in relation to the number of technicians.

If the need for responsiveness (low mean response time) is the dominant issue, it is best not to use an account representative relationship.

Third-Party Service Providers

A major strategic decision facing nearly all manufacturers is the decision regarding which party will provide the labor and parts support for a product in the field. Many larger companies have found that the best approach here is to provide the service themselves through a field service division. However, with increasing costs, increasing reliability, and decreasing revenues, many smaller and medium-sized companies are finding that it is more cost effective to turn to third-party and/or fourth-party service providers for some or all of their service support strategy. (Fourth-party service providers typically provide service to second- and third-party service organizations.)

The advantage of a third-party service (TPS) provider is that the TPS already has technicians in the area and can provide coverage for a relatively small machine population. The disadvantage of the TPS is that the manufacturer may lose some control over the service experience, may lose an opportunity to be close to the customer, may miss some customer feedback information that could help in improving the product design, and may lose some opportunities to sell complementary products, service agreements, and/or equipment. (Some people call this "losing account control.")

Caution must also be taken that the third-party service provider does not become spread too thin and lose focus. When this happens, service quality quickly declines.

A typical TPS agreement calls for the TPS organization to subcontract the complete delivery of service for a particular product. It is also possible to subcontract the "labor only" portion of the field service where the manufacturer continues to manage the parts side of the business.

Fourth-party services provide parts and/or depot service for both third-party and self-maintainer organizations. Fourth-party services often have lower prices and are more responsive than original equipment manufacturers. However, some argue that original equipment manufacturers will have better quality and better access to the schematics that are necessary for installation and repair.

Organizational Reporting Relationship

Should the field service organization report to manufacturing, marketing, sales, distribution/logistics, or information systems, or should it be a separate division? This question is not an easy one to answer. It is clear that field service performs some marketing/sales functions, needs to communicate with manufacturing concerning parts, and performs a distribution function. Many manufacturing companies have organized field service as a separate entity because field service business is very different from other organizational units.

Complementary Products

The idea of complementary products is well-known in both the marketing and the operations management literature. The idea is relatively new to the field service industry. A cleverly assembled complementary bundle of products and services can offer so much value to the customer that the customer will become extremely loyal. The service provider does so much total customer care that the provider almost owns the customer in this type of relationship. This concept may be particularly useful for field service organizations that are experiencing the downward spiral (mentioned later in this chapter) of declining revenues and increasing costs. The concept is fleshed out in a field service context by the field service organization providing more than just field service. The field service organization can be viewed as the contact point for the entire customer/supplier relationship and can be used as the entree for professional consulting services, facility management services, educational programs, sales of other related products, sales of software related to the products, and so on.

POPULATION DENSITY AND THE DOWNWARD SPIRAL

Some companies have found themselves in a downward spiral regarding response times and machine density. As the machine population declines and/or as failure rates decline, field service management reduces the number of technicians. With fewer technicians, response times get longer and field service gets worse. Customers find the service unsatisfactory and defect to the competitor's products or use third- or fourth-party service providers. The result is a downward spiral that ultimately leads to the company turning the service of its products over to a third-party service or getting out of the service business all together. No easy solutions to this spiral are known. However, the following ideas might be of some help:

- Understand that machine density is the key to response times. This suggests that the service provider should attempt to attract customers that are close together and control the expectations for customers that are further away from the high-density areas.
- Be very careful with technician morale. Communicate with the technicians and be careful to avoid surprises regarding layoffs.
- If a significant reduction in the number of technicians is necessary, try to focus the product line so that training costs and parts

can be kept to a reasonable level. On the other hand, it may be possible for the company to introduce new products that will maintain the critical mass of technicians necessary for the field service organization to survive.

CONCLUSIONS

Field service strategy is a much neglected area. However, the stress caused by declining profits is forcing many managers to reevaluate their assumptions and rethink the role that their field service strategy plays in their overall business strategy.

This chapter challenges the traditional view that field service is simply a technical area with little strategic importance. Field service personnel are often the *only* people from the service provider's organization who have regular contact with the customer. This close relationship can be used for powerful advantage to position the product, reduce the consumer's perception of risk, gain market intelligence, communicate a positive image for the company, sell complementary products, improve product quality, and improve manufacturing conformance quality.

This chapter also suggests that a field service strategy should consider alternatives such as service guarantees, high-density market strategies, third-party service providers, and joint ventures. These alternatives seem to be particularly important during times of economic stress.

In conclusion, field service strategy should not and cannot be ignored. A good field service strategy can make the difference between thriving and failing in today's competitive marketplace.

CHAPTER 3

PERFORMANCE MEASUREMENT FOR FIELD SERVICE: MANAGING BY THE NUMBERS

INTRODUCTION

A good field service manager expects and demands continuous performance improvement. Complacency is not acceptable in this day of rapid technological and economic change. A good performance measurement system is critical to assessing the progress along the path of continuous improvement.

A good performance measurement system also supports many important field service management activities including:

- Staffing for technicians in the field, TAC (Technical Assistance Center) technicians, and dispatchers.
- Reassigning of technicians to other territories.
- Training of technicians and dispatchers.
- Total inventory investment.
- Inventory allocations in the field.
- Pay, incentives, and promotion.
- Evaluation of accounts for profitability.
- Pricing of parts, service contracts, and time and materials calls.
- Billing for time and materials service calls.

The design of the performance measurement system is critical to field service strategy. The success of the field service organization has much to do with the degree to which the performance measurement system matches the field service strategy and the degree to which the performance measurements motivate the field service workforce to support that strategy.

Unfortunately, field service performance measures do not always work as expected. It is easy for field service managers to "shoot themselves in the foot" by using inappropriate performance measures. For example, it seems reasonable to measure the number of times that a technican is called back to repair a machine within two days. However, this measure gives technicians incentive to wait as long as they can to clear the call (report that the repair is complete). This measure also encourages technicians to ask the customer to call them personally rather than report the call to the dispatcher. In some cases, this measure may even encourage the technician to spend too much time on a call.

This chapter will present and evaluate a number of performance measures used by many field service organizations. The chapter is organized into three major sections:

- Financial performance measures.
- Service call performance measures.
- Service parts performance measures.

The chapter concludes with a brief description of some of the data collection problems that confound field service performance measurement systems.

The concepts of customer surveys and benchmarking are also very important methods for measuring performance. They are relatively new approaches for field service businesses and are both related to quality management. These subjects will be addressed in the Service Quality Management chapter.

FINANCIAL PERFORMANCE MEASURES

Revenues

Direct sources of revenues include service agreements, time and materials calls, and service parts. Indirect revenues come from repeat sales of equipment, sales of facilitating goods (software, etc.), and sales of training materials and courses. Revenues may be broken down by region, area, territory, account, and technician. Parts and labor-related revenues may also be broken out separately. Field service revenues can make a significant contribution to a company's bottom line.

Cost

Field service costs can be very significant. Costs include technician and dispatcher labor, parts, vehicles, tools (often purchased by the technicians), and very significant overhead costs for carrying inventory, computer support, telecommunications, management, offices, and so forth. Costs can be broken down by region, area, territory, and account.

With very large overhead costs, field service organizations allocate large amounts of overhead to technician labor. Field service managers must be very careful with these allocated costs. For example, one service organization tried to justify an artificial intelligence "call-avoidance" system on the basis of a fully burdened, technician cost of $250 per hour. This analysis is incorrect. Reducing the number of service calls by 10 percent will not save the company 10 percent of the fully burdened technician labor cost. (Nearly all of the overhead will still be there with a reduction of 10 percent of the technician labor force.) At most, the company would save 10 percent of the unburdened-technician labor cost—and even that is questionable, given the fact that some areas still need to be covered even though technician utilization may be lower.

Profitability

Many companies measure profitability (or at least gross margin) by product, by region, by technician, by customer, by account, by machine, and so on. As noted in the strategy chapter, profitability can lead to problems because it is so myopic. Warranty repair is extremely important to the long-term success of most service organizations; yet, warranty repair is not profitable—at least not from a narrow field service view.

IBM has made an interesting move by focusing more on total revenues and profits for both products and services. IBM recognizes that services have a higher margin (25 to 45 percent) than products (8 to 15 percent) and that it is necessary to consider them together rather than separately.

Obviously, financial performance is extremely important. The point here is that short-term financial performance does not provide a complete picture of the effectiveness of a field service organization. Many other performance measures are essential to an accurate field service performance evaluation. Many of these are discussed below.

SERVICE CALL PERFORMANCE MEASURES

The following is a list of measures that may be used to evaluate system performance related to service calls. These measures relate primarily to technicians, but also reflect the performance of training programs, staffing levels, dispatching decisions, and machine reliability.

Response Time

For many managers, mean response time is the most important measure of performance. Although the mean response time is a convenient measure, it is flawed for several reasons.

First, mean response time is not a good measure of overall performance because the tail of the response time distribution has much more effect on customer satisfaction than does the mean. The median is regarded as a better measure of central tendency than the mean. The median is the "middle" value and is found by ranking the values and taking the middle value from the list.

For example, the following service call data has been ranked by response time:

Service Call:	1	2	3	4	5	6	7	8	9
Response Time:	1	2	4	6	7	7	10	15	66

The mean value here is 13.1, whereas the median value is 7. The value "66" is an "outlier" and is not representative of the other values. It may be a data entry error or some unusual situation (e.g., the call was in a remote area of Texas that was inaccessible because of a flood). The median is considered to be an "error resistant" statistic (a statistic that is not sensitive to either outliers or errors in the data), whereas the mean is not. This brings to mind the story of the frog that has one foot in icy water and the other in boiling water. This frog is "happy on average."

Second, neither the mean nor the median directly measures how long the tail of the distribution is. In many service businesses, it is unsatisfactory to have 20 percent of the customers with a 20-hour response time even though the mean may be only three hours. This will happen if many service calls have a response time much less than three hours.

Third, the mean response time does not tell us very much when the response time expectations are not the same for all customers and all service calls. Even a short response time may not be short enough if it does not meet the customer's expectations based on a service agreement or a business requirement. Response time should be measured with respect to customer expectations rather than as a simple average across all service calls.

Percent Uptime (or Percent Availability)

The percent of the time that a machine is fully operational is an important measure for many customers. Unfortunately, for many service providers, this measure is difficult to derive because the service provider must know the customer's hours of operation and must also have a clear idea of the severity of the problem. Sometimes a machine may have a "soft down," which does not directly affect machine performance. "Average Machine Downtime per Failure" and "Percent Downtime" are similar measures.

Percent of Calls on Time

The percent of calls that are on time with respect to some target response time can be a useful performance measurement. However, it is important to determine the "target" response time that makes sense for the customer. The following factors should be considered when determining the target response time for a service call:

Customer—An important customer might have a lower target response time.

Customer contract—A contract might specify the target (or required) response time.

Machine/model—A more important machine might have a shorter target response time. (Medical machines generally have a shorter target response time than do copy machines.)

Urgency of the particular service call—A customer crying for help might have a shorter target response time.

Location of the customer site—A customer closer to the technician (or the branch office) might have a shorter target response time.

If the customer is aware of the target response time, this serves as a surrogate measure of how well the actual response time meets customer expectations.

A very similar measure is "average tardiness" where tardiness is the number of hours that the response time exceeds the response time target. In other words, average tardiness is the average lateness for those calls that are late. This measure is rarely used in industry but has long been discussed and applied in research studies. It can be extended by giving customers nonequal weights (tardiness for some customers is more important than it is for others) and/or by adding the square of the tardiness (two hours tardy is much worse than one hour tardy).

First Call Effectiveness

The percent of service calls that require a second site visit within X hours or days. (This can be measured as a percentage or as the number of service calls.) Some companies call this the "percent of return calls" or "short-interval" calls. Technicians are often called back to a customer site within one to seven days after a repair. Obviously, service providers want to "do it right the first time" so as to minimize these return calls. Most agree that this measure is more important than the mean time to repair.

However, this measurement has a serious drawback in that technicians may try to wait to close a call until after the machine has been operational for serveral hours or even a day or two. Management needs to make sure that the reporting system does not allow this to happen.

Percent of Service Calls That Make the Target Technician Telephone Response Time

Some service organizations require that a technician call the customer back within X minutes of the time that the customer reported the machine failure. At National Computer Systems this is called the "commit time" and is set at 60 minutes. This policy has several advantages:

- It gives the customer the chance to get some immediate attention from a trained technician.
- The customer's perception is that they are now really in the system and that someone has made a solid, personal commitment to come help them with their problem.
- The technician gives the customer a reliable, estimated time of arrival so that the customer can plan around the machine failure. No one can give a better estimated time of arrival than the technician who will actually be working on the machine.

Number of No-Parts Calls (Parts Unavailable Calls)

A no-parts call is one that cannot be completed due to the fact that the required parts are not available when the technician needs them. No-parts calls typically mean extended downtimes compared to other service calls. The cost of a no-parts call is very high. This includes the cost of returning to the site again, obtaining the part (often via express mail), lost customer goodwill, wasted labor, dispatching, communications, etc.

Number of No-Material-Used Calls

The number of calls that do not require any materials or parts; repairs can sometimes be made via phone consultation.

Number of Calls Completed the Same Day

In several customer surveys, it has been found that many customers expect a machine to be fixed the same day that the service call was reported (at least if the machine failed in the early or middle part of the day). This is an interesting and potentially important measure, but it is not used by very many service organizations.

Number of No-Trouble-Found Calls

A no-trouble-found situation occurs when the technician is unable to find any problem with the machine. An intermittent machine problem is often the cause.

Technician Utilization

Utilization is defined as the percent of the work hours that a technician is actually in transit to a call or working on a machine. Service organizations must be very careful with utilization. Response time increases very quickly as utilization approaches 100 percent. The goal is to find the right utilization that provides a good balance between labor cost and service. Overemphasis on utilization can easily lead to technicians simply reporting longer travel times and longer machine repair times. Technician utilization is a useful measure of overall system performance and certainly has value in determining staffing levels. However, utilization should not be used as a performance measurement for evaluating technicians. Field service management should get excited about the things that excite the customer (e.g., uptime, meeting expectations, response time, etc.).

Time to Repair

The time spent to repair machines in the field is often used to measure performance. The mean time to repair (MTTR), which is estimated by reliability engineers before the product is sold, may not match the MTTR experienced in the field. This is due to unexpected operator behavior or operating conditions (dirt, humidity, and so forth).

The time to repair has many problems as a performance measure. These include:

- Expert technicians are often given the very difficult machines and, therefore, might have a longer MTTR.
- If MTTR is used as a performance measure, technicians might try to avoid difficult machines and sacrifice customer satisfaction in the process.

- If technicians are told to improve the MTTR, they are motivated to cut corners in the repair and therefore will increase the frequency of return to the site to repair the machine again. (Technicians will also cut corners on the face-to-face time for training and customer relations.) It is better to do the job right the first time. Customers are probably more concerned about response time, uptime, and frequency of failures than the mean time to repair.

When used with caution, MTTR can be a useful tool for gaining a better understanding of the performance of one or more technicians or machines.

Direct Labor Hours per Machine per Quarter

This measure is very similar to the MTTR except that it includes travel time. It can be used as a surrogate measure of the overall profitability for a group of machines or technicians.

Number of Calls per Machine per Quarter

Digital Equipment Corporation uses this as an overall measure of the quality of service. It directly relates to profitability for a particular type of equipment and/or group of technicians. It also gets away from many of the reporting accuracy issues that arise with a number of the other measures. This measure is best for situations with an account representative relationship between the technicians and the accounts. This measure has the same problem as the percent of return calls (or number of return calls) in that technicians may take a "hit" on their performance measure if they close a call and then have to return to repair the machine shortly thereafter. (Note that this measure is the inverse of the mean time between failure [MTBF].)

Repeat Business

According to Kellogg, Rose, and Chase (1991), a measure of repeat business may also be useful. In some sense, the ultimate test of a customer's satisfaction with service is the decision to renew a service agreement (or similarly to buy a service agreement upon expiration of the warranty service period or to purchase another machine). This may be measured as the percent of customers that renew/buy a service agreement.

Phone Statistics

A large number of ACD (automatic call distribution) system telephone statistics are readily available to measure the performance of the people who are receiving phone calls from customers and/or technicians. Some of these include:

Number of calls arriving per time period.

Mean and distribution of delay time (hold time).

Number of times that customers abandoned the phone call.

Mean and distribution of talk time.

Time available (as determined by the system).

Mean and distribution of wrap-up time.

Most ACD systems make all of these measures available by time of day (e.g., 15-minute time periods). These measures are very useful for staffing and ACD design decisions. However, there is some danger in using some of these—particularly talk time. If individual dispatchers are evaluated on the basis of average talk time, they may be tempted to rush the customer (or technician) and not provide a satisfactory service. The goal is customer satisfaction—not short talk times. On the other hand, some measure of overall talk time may be useful to management for indicating a need for training in a particular area.

Delay time (hold time) is probably the most important measure as it is a good reflection of the balance between staffing and demand. A long delay time does not necessarily mean that the dispatchers should have shorter talk times; a better solution may be to staff more dispatchers during that time of the day.

The typical industry approach to measuring average delay time is to include *only* those calls that have a nonzero delay. For example, given five hold times (0, 0, 0, 20, 40), the averag delay time is 30 seconds. The best way to define a delay-time policy is in terms of the percent of calls that have to wait more than X seconds. (This is called the "grade-of-service" in the industry.) For example, one company specifies that 80 percent of all incoming calls should not have to wait more than 20 seconds before the customer has the opportunity to talk to a human being.

The distribution of delay times is useful for studying abandoned calls (people who get tired of waiting and hang up the phone). The point at which the distribution takes a distinct drop (the "knee" of the curve) is a good indication of the time that people are abandoning the call.

Many systems measure the after-call "wrap-up" work time. This is the time that the dispatcher needs to wrap up the transaction after hanging up the phone. When the dispatcher hangs up the phone, the system automatically considers the dispatcher in the wrap-up phone status until the dispatcher hits the available button on the phone. Wrap-up time can be an important issue in both queuing studies and in performance improvement programs.

The percent of time that the dispatchers are signed on (either available or talking with customers) is a good performance measure. Dispatchers cannot control the number of incoming calls, but they can control the percent of time they work that day. This is called the "clock-time" report in some ACD systems.

Other Measures
Other measures that can be used include: percent of preventive maintenance calls completed on time, number of site visits, number of engineers on a call, and number of calls requiring escalation.[1]

SERVICE PARTS PERFORMANCE MEASURES

Service parts inventory performance can be measured in terms of both service and inventory investment performance. Each of these is discussed below. Financial issues were discussed previously.

Percent of Orders Shipped the Same Day
This measure is widely used. Similar measures can be developed for special orders (rush orders) and for other types of orders.

---

[1] Many of these were contributed by Fred Van Bennekom of Boston University.

Order–Fill Accuracy

This is the percent of orders that are filled correctly in terms of part numbers, quantities, and so forth.

Total Inventory Investment

This is an aggregate measurement of inventory performance. Obviously, this can be broken down by commodity classes, models, and so forth.

Inventory Turnover

This commonly used measure is usually computed as the annual sales/average inventory investment. Field service companies, by necessity, carry many items that are very slow moving. As a result, most field service inventories have an annual turnover of around 1.5 turns per year. This is poor by most manufacturing and distribution system standards, but is typical for a service parts inventory.

Average Number of Days of Supply in Inventory

This is the average number of days of supply across all parts in the inventory and is a good measure of obsolescence. This is closely related to turnover.

No-Parts Calls

This is the percent of calls that cannot be completed due to lack of parts. This is, therefore, a measure of the effectiveness of the inventory stocking policies for the technicians' vehicles.

Age of Backorders

This can be expressed as a distribution that shows the number of orders that have gone unfilled for 0 to 30 days, 31 to 60 days, 61 to 90 days, and over 90 days. Sometimes orders are not filled immediately because the items are not on hand. Sometimes orders are onetime problems with suppliers or somehow slip through the system and are never ordered. This measure can be defined for backorders to customers and/or backorders for replenishment for technicians.

Average Repair Shop Time

This is the average flow time for a repairable part to be processed through the repair shop. It includes the queue time as well as the actual time being repaired. When parts can be repaired faster, a smaller inventory is required.

DATA COLLECTION PROCEDURES
FOR PERFORMANCE MEASUREMENT

Internal performance measures are often based on data collected from technicians. Technicians typically collect information such as service call number, model/serial, customer name/ID, departure time, travel time, arrival time, repair time, departure time, materials used, problems found, and so on. The following are principles that should guide field service data collection efforts:

- Technicians are professionals and should be given feedback on their performance so that they can improve themselves. Information should not be used as a club but as a teacher, not as a weapon of destruction but as a tool for self-improvement. If this philosophy is not adopted, technician morale will suffer and they might devise ways to get around the system.
- Unnecessary data collection should be eliminated. If the data do not add value, do not collect it. (This is one of the basic tenants of the "just-in-time" philosophy.) One technician complained to the author that his company required technicians to collect extensive information on problem causes for all models. This information was given to the design engineering group. Unfortunately, several models that this technician repaired were no longer being manufactured and this information was simply thrown away.
- Do not expect technicians to be accurate when they are self-reporting all of their times. Times will only be accurate if there is some validity checking, such as requiring technicians to call the dispatcher when they arrive at the customer's site, making

sure that the reported times are consistent with one another, and so on. Human memory is extremely biased and fallible.

- Hand-held, notebook computer, and communication technologies now make it possible for technicians to enter data remotely. These devices can ensure accurate times for all activities because they can time-stamp all transactions. This technology also makes it fairly easy for technicians to accept and clear service calls without talking directly to a dispatcher. However, some people question the wisdom of managing technicians without some verbal communication with the service organization home office.

CONCLUSIONS

It is well known that performance measurement plays a critical role in supporting the field service strategy. Given the nature of human behavior, the performance measurement system almost *becomes* the field service strategy. This chapter has pointed out the dangers of many commonly used measures and has recommended several measures that might be useful in some field service organizations.

People often respond in the same manner that they are treated. If management treats employees as an adversary, employees will probably respond in an adversarial way. If treated as professionals who want to satisfy the customer just as much as anyone else, they will generally respond in a positive way. Management's role is to provide the support employees need to do their job. Management should be frequently asking the question, "What can we do to help you do your job better?" Management must then listen carefully and respond with definite actions. Given this philosophical foundation, technicians and others are freed up to understand that data collection and performance measurement are necessary to help the service organization continuously improve itself.

The performance measurements in this chapter have been entirely internal measures—measures derived from the service organization's own internal data. The next chapter presents the concepts of customer surveys and benchmarking which are external measurements. These concepts will be discussed in the context of field service quality improvement.

CHAPTER 4

SERVICE QUALITY MANAGEMENT: MANAGING CUSTOMER SATISFACTION

INTRODUCTION

Service quality is a hot topic today. However, few people seem to have a clear operational definition of service quality. For example, people have equated service quality with:

- Extra services.
- Lots of inspection.
- Performance measurement.
- Average response time.
- Good interpersonal relationships with customers.
- Zero defects.
- Do it right the first time.

While all of these are important issues related to quality management, they are all bad definitions of quality.

The concepts of quality and of satisfying customer expectations permeate this entire book. However, this chapter focuses on several critical service quality topics essential to managing a field service organization. These topics include:

- Service Quality—How to understand service quality with the "gap" model.
- Service Recovery—How to rescue bad situations so that customers do not defect.

- Customer Surveys—How to find out how your customers perceive your field service performance.
- Benchmarking—How to identify, analyze, and adapt industry-best practices that can lead to superior performance.

We begin with a simple definition of what quality is in a field service context.

SERVICE QUALITY

Parasuraman, Zeithaml, and Berry define service quality from the customer's view rather than based on internal performance measures. From this perspective, *service quality* is the customer's perception of the superiority of the service. *Satisfaction* is defined as a customer's *perception* of a single service experience, whereas *quality* is the accumulation of the satisfaction for many customers over many service experiences. A quality service provider is one that is able to consistently provide a satisfying service experience over a long period of time.[2]

A customer's satisfaction with a field service experience results from a comparison of expectations before the service experience to the perception of the actual service experience. As mentioned in the introductory chapter, this concept can be stated in a pseudomathematical way as:

Service quality = Satisfaction with service delivery
= Perceived service delivery − Expected service delivery
= P − E

Perceived service delivery *(P)* is the customer's perception of the service actually received. It is possible that the customer's perception of the service may be different from the reality because the customer may not know all of the facts or may have misinterpreted the facts. Perceptions of the actual delivery are also heavily influenced by the service

---

[2]Teas (1991) criticizes the P − E model and offers another approach for measuring service quality.

process as well as the service result. For example, a very short down-time experience may not be perceived as a good service if the technician is rude to the user.

Expected service delivery *(E)* is what the customer feels that the service provider *should* provide. It is not a prediction of what the customer thinks the service provider *will* provide. Expectations are derived from many sources. In a field service context, the customer derives expectations from the warranty or service agreement, past experiences with many service providers, promises made by dispatchers and technicians, and many other sources.

The difference between P and E measures the degree and direction of the discrepancy between the customer's perceptions and expectations. The measure $P - E$, therefore, is a measure of customer satisfaction with a particular service experience. When taken over many service experiences, it can become a measure of overall service quality.

Field service management must, therefore, manage *both* the actual delivery of the service experience and the expectations that are created before the service experience occurs. It is not enough to manage only the delivery.

This gap between P and E can be measured by means of a survey instrument. Zeithaml, Parasuraman, and Berry's book, *Delivering Quality Service*, presents a 22-question survey that can be adapted for field service. The survey has two sections—one that deals with expectations and one that deals with perceptions (evaluations) of the actual delivery. The research by the authors suggests that a gap greater than one (on a seven-point scale for all items on the survey) is probably not an acceptable gap. These issues are discussed further in this chapter in the section on surveys.

Some research has suggested that service quality can be broken down into two types: quality for normal service needs and quality for exceptional service needs. A service organization that can handle normal service requirements but is unable and/or unwilling to handle customer emergencies will probably not be viewed as a high quality service provider.

Several studies have found that the biggest complaint with field service, in general, is that the customer's time expectations are not being satisfied. A big problem for many service companies is managing the customer's expectations regarding response time—and managing response time itself—so that the two match up in such a way that the customer is completely satisfied. The concept of "no surprises" is an important one in nearly all business dealings.

One of the most fundamental issues in closing the service quality gap is the empowerment of the service contact employees (dispatchers and technicians) to use discretion in meeting customer expectations. Empowerment of employees means giving them authority to get involved in the service recovery process (described below). The benefits of empowered employees are significant. Empowered employees can often turn an irate customer who is ready to defect (and give a bad report to 20 other people) into a loyal, satisfied customer. Of course, management needs to set limits on what the service contact employee can do and should provide training in how to deal creatively with customers. The next section develops these concepts more completely.

SERVICE RECOVERY

An important emerging concept from the service operations management literature is the concept of "service recovery." Service recovery is what you do to remedy a "service failure." A service failure is any incident on which the customer's expectations have not been satisfied. A service failure occurs every time a technician does not make a promised arrival time, every time a promise is broken regarding returning a call, etc.

Many organizations do not have any formal service recovery process. The result is that service failures are often ignored or, at best, handled inconsistently. Thus, many customers end up defecting to the competition, often without giving a reason to the service organization. It is much easier to keep a customer than to win a new one. Whereas satisfied customers tell a few others about their good service, dissatisfied customers often tell *many* others. The average number of people who directly hear that bad report is often estimated to be in the range of 10 to 20 people. The average number who receive the bad report second-hand is probably much larger.

One of the most fascinating and significant facts about service recovery is that customers who experience a service failure and experience a good service recovery are often *more* loyal than customers who have never had a service failure in the first place. This suggests that the service failure tested the relationship and the service provider had an opportunity to provide a serious commitment to that customer via the service recovery process.

It seems clear that companies with a good service recovery process benefit by retaining customers, building customer loyalty, and avoiding ex-customers who spread bad reports. On the other hand, organizations without a good service recovery system lose customers, miss opportunities to build loyalty, have ex-customers spreading bad reports, and probably spend too much money on uneven handling of service failures.

The following service recovery process is built on the article by Hart, Heskett, and Sasser:

Apology.   Immediately acknowledge the error. Do not try to make excuses for the failure. If you are guilty, then take full responsibility for the problem. Even if you are not guilty, at least listen and try to find some reasonable apology.

Urgent Reinstatement.   Do the best job that you can to get things back to status quo. A big part of this is the demonstration that the service provider has the customer's best interests at heart. A very useful question to ask here is, "What can we do to satisfy you completely in this situation?"

Empathy.   Empathy is not the same as sympathy. Empathy is showing compassion for the person in pain without personally feeling the pain, whereas sympathy feels the person's pain. Empathy is appropriate, but sympathy is not. In this case, it may be appropriate to say something like, "I can understand how you must feel."

Symbolic Atonement.   Give the customer some sort of meaningful symbol to demonstrate the organization's commitment. Customers are often easily satisfied. The customer usually does not need or want an inappropriately large gift. Often the customer only wants some sort of expression of the service organization's care, concern, and loyalty.

Follow-up.   Ideally, the technician or a service manager should call the "victim" to make sure that everything is okay.

The above steps are a good foundation for the design of a service recovery process, but the service recovery requires more than these steps. It is necessary to define policies (e.g., what sort of symbolic atonement is to be provided), information systems (e.g., keep track of response time promises and measure performance against these), and formal training programs.

CUSTOMER SURVEYS

A good customer survey can measure performance from the customer's perspective. This perspective is clearly more valid than any of the internal measures presented in the chapter on performance measurement. This concept is relatively new and is becoming very popular.

The technique is very simple. A random sample of customer repair experiences is surveyed in order to ascertain how well the service organization is performing on a number of dimensions such as:

- Call takers/dispatchers—telephone hold-time.
- Technical assistance center—helpfulness.
- Technicians—response time, meeting promised arrival time, repair time, availability of parts, adequacy of the repair.
- Overall customer satisfaction.

Some companies survey both importance and satisfaction on each variable and then measure the gap between the two. As mentioned earlier, the book *Delivering Quality Service* by Zeithaml, Parasuraman, and Berry presents a well-tested survey instrument and methodology for conducting such a survey. They suggest that questions be organized into five dimensions: tangibles, reliability, responsiveness, assurance, and empathy. They explain these dimensions in detail and give several survey items (questions) to be used for each dimension.

While most organizations use a mail survey, many service organizations have discovered the power of using a phone survey instead. The advantages of a phone survey include:

- Relatively low cost. Dispatching personnel can conduct phone surveys during the slow times of the work day. A mail survey is probably less expensive per customer surveyed, but is probably more expensive per customer response and has a lower return on the investment in terms of the quality of the data obtained.

- Learning. Dispatchers can benefit from hearing customers evaluate the field service performance. Dispatchers get direct feedback from the customer that helps them make the difficult tradeoffs in the future.

- Good response rate. End-users are much more likely to respond to a person requesting information on the telephone than they are to a survey form received in the mail.

- Timely data. The end-user can be called just as soon as the service call is closed. Nearly all service organizations that have conducted mail surveys have horror stories about how customers forgot the details after just a few days. For example, one manager tells the story of following up on a survey that reported poor service from a technician. Upon calling the customer, the manager discovered that the customer had confused two service companies and that the poor service was from a different company. If time delay had been shorter, this error would be less likely to occur.

- Right person. It is more likely that the phone call will get to the correct end-user/operator than will a typical mail survey form. (Some argue that whoever decides on the service contract purchase is the right person.) Mail surveys are generally sent to the accounts payable department or to the individual who requested the service rather than the person who actually operates the machine.

- Data analysis. Once an interactive computer system is set up for the surveys, the data for the service call can be kept as a part of the record for that call. Data from mail surveys often have to be manually entered into the computer and the computer must perform a search in order to match the survey with the service call record.

- Customized questions. With a computer interface, phone surveys can be easily customized to the specific hardware repaired on the service call. A computer-based system makes it possible for management to pursue information about specific models, technicians, or customers.

Sample size calculations for surveys are fairly simple to compute. Managers are often interested in computing the sample size N that is necessary to estimate a percentage, such as the percentage of customers who are satisfied. Appendix 4.1 presents a method for computing appropriate values for N to achieve management objectives.

No matter how the survey is implemented, surveys can and should play an important role as an external performance standard. These surveys should not be a onetime event, but rather an ongoing process that provides management with a "thermometer" that can be used to measure the health of the service delivery system on an ongoing (longitudinal) basis.

BENCHMARKING

Benchmarking attempts to answer the following questions about products and/or services:

1. Is the competition (or anyone else) better than we are? If so, then by how much?
2. Why are they better?
3. What lessons can we learn from them?
4. How can we apply what we have learned?

Xerox and Ford credit benchmarking concepts with practically saving their companies. Many other companies have found benchmarking to be extremely useful in measuring and improving both quality and productivity. The concept of benchmarking has been around for many years. For example, the Japanese automotive industry "innovatively imitated" Ford's assembly line concept and Ford imitated the Sears mail-order plant. Although seemingly forgotten in the United States and Europe, the concept has recently been rediscovered and is quickly gaining popularity.

Many organizations foolishly measure their performance only against their own historical performance rather than against some objective external standard. As a result, these organizations expend their energies working on small incremental improvements on a process that is far inferior to the best possible process. Benchmarking forces management to focus on external rather than on internal standards. This often stresses the organization in a positive way to think about radical, new technologies and about what can be rather than just what is. Benchmarking can help management identify quality and productivity gaps and help prioritize process improvement programs.

A critical prerequisite to benchmarking is a clear understanding of how customers define quality. This should be derived from customer surveys as discussed above. Benchmarks must be defined in terms of the variables important to the customer.

The three distinct types of benchmarking include:

Competitive benchmarking.
Noncompetitive benchmarking.
Internal benchmarking.

Each of these types of benchmarking is discussed below.

Competitive Benchmarking. Seeks to compare company performance against the best-in-class performance. If the study does find that competitors produce a superior service, "innovative imitation" should take place to improve the service. If, on the other hand, the company finds that it is already providing superior service, it might advertise to exploit this advantage in the marketplace. The benchmarking process should carefully define both the measurement scale (variable) and the standard on that scale.

Noncompetitive Benchmarking. Studies best-of-class performance in a specific business function. For example, Xerox wanted to study billing practices, so they went outside their industry and found that Federal Express was the best-of-class in billing systems. Xerox then innovatively imitated the Federal Express billing system and adapted it to their own needs. In only comparing itself to its competitors and to others in the same industry, a company might miss out on an opportunity to "leapfrog" its competition.

Internal Benchmarking.   Refers to improvements within an organization over time. Often the benchmarks are based on performance of leading plants, divisions, or product lines.

No matter what type of benchmarking is done, the benchmarking study should include a careful analysis of the processes that are in use. The goal of benchmarking is not just setting standards—it is setting standards *and* documenting processes so that process improvements can be made.

Some consulting companies (e.g., Coopers & Lybrand, International, Prognostics) provide benchmark information to field service organizations. Many organizations are finding that simply hosting guests from other companies (usually noncompetitors in the same industry) can help them informally benchmark and improve their performance. Professional societies, software vendors, and consultants can often provide some insightful benchmark information as well. Motorola and Xerox offer training programs that many organizations have found useful.

Some cautionary notes are appropriate here. In a rapidly changing industry, it is difficult to establish useful benchmarks. By the time the benchmarks are established, the industry has moved on to a new technology or a new strategy. If done correctly, benchmarking may be very expensive. There may be some legal obstacles to some forms of competitive benchmarking. Benchmarking often requires that the organization be open to sharing data with benchmarking partners.

Clearly, benchmarking has been a powerful concept in many industries. Benchmarking for field service will increase dramatically in importance in the near future.

CONCLUSIONS

Service quality is much more than a faddish new emphasis on performance measurement. Service quality is defined as an accumulation of customer perceptions of service experiences—either satisfying or nonsatisfying experiences. Customer satisfaction is based on the gap between the customer's perception of the actual delivery and expected delivery.

When the actual service delivery is less than what was expected, the service provider should have a formal service recovery system in place in order to maintain customer loyalty. It is far easier to restore a customer than to win a new one.

Customer surveys are a powerful method for ascertaining customer perceptions of service performance and satisfaction. While internal measures such as average response time can give management some insight into system performance, customer surveys can provide an external measure of the most important output of the system—customer satisfaction.

Benchmarking is also a powerful method for objectively measuring performance. Benchmarking is much more than comparing overall performance to that of another organization. Benchmarks can be established for each business process and, when superior processes are identified, the processes can be creatively copied. This is an excellent way to facilitate learning for a field service organization.

Both customer surveys and benchmarking are essential for setting external standards for service quality and for directing performance improvement efforts. In the absence of external measures, it is very easy for a field service organization to become nonchalant and move very slowly along the path of continuous improvement.

Finally, field service plays an important role in overall quality in the larger organization. For example, field service can and should be heavily involved in providing feedback for improving both design and conformance quality.

Appendix 4.1   SAMPLE SIZE CALCULATION FOR SURVEYS

Managers are often interested in computing the sample size N that is necessary to estimate a percentage such as the percentage of customers that are satisfied. The goal is to create a confidence interval that contains the true percentage.

A confidence interval is defined as a percentage p plus or minus h percent where h is usually around 5 percent ($h = 0.05$). The probability that the confidence interval "contains" the true percentage is $(1 - \alpha)$ where $(1 - \alpha)$ is usually set to around 95.5%.

The sample size can be computed from the equation below or from Table 4–1. The standard sample size calculation is as follows:

$$N = z^2 p(1 - p)/h^2$$

where,

  N = Recommended sample size.

  z = Standard normal deviate. A value of $z = 2$ will provide a 95.5% confidence interval ($\alpha = 0.0225$).

  p = Estimated percent made before the sample is taken. The closer that p is to .5 the larger the value of $p(1 - p)$ and the larger the sample size. If no estimate of the percentage is known before hand, a value of $p = .5$ is recommended to be conservative.

  h = Half-width of the confidence interval. We suggest a value of 5 percent here. The smaller this value is, the larger the required sample size. The sample size calculation is very sensitive to the value.

The sample size calculation procedure is as follows:

1. Set z and h based on the desired size of the confidence interval.
2. Estimate p from a preliminary sample or from past data. Use $p = .5$ if no past data are available.
3. Calculate N based on z, p, and h using the above equation. Be sure to round up to be conservative.
4. Collect N sample observations.
5. Calculate the sample percentage p from the sample data.
6. Recompute N based on the new sample percentage and take further observations if needed. (This last step is often omitted.)

For example, the last survey found that about 70 percent of the customers were very satisfied. How many observations are needed to get a 95 percent confidence interval on the true percentage with a half

TABLE 4–1
Sample Size Calculation (N) for a 95.5 Percent Confidence Interval*

Half-width (h)	Estimated Percentage (p)									
	0.95	0.90	0.85	0.80	0.75	0.70	0.65	0.60	0.55	0.50
0.100	19	36	51	64	75	84	91	96	99	100
0.095	22	40	57	71	84	94	101	107	110	111
0.090	24	45	63	80	93	104	113	119	123	124
0.085	27	50	71	89	104	117	126	133	138	139
0.080	30	57	80	100	118	132	143	150	155	157
0.075	34	64	91	114	134	150	162	171	176	178
0.070	39	74	105	131	154	172	186	196	203	205
0.065	45	86	121	152	178	199	216	228	235	237
0.060	53	100	142	178	209	234	250	267	275	278
0.055	63	120	169	212	248	278	301	318	328	331
0.050	76	144	204	256	300	336	364	384	396	400
0.045	94	178	252	317	371	415	450	475	489	494
0.040	119	225	319	400	469	525	569	600	619	625
0.035	156	294	417	523	613	686	743	784	809	817
0.030	212	400	567	712	834	934	1,012	1,067	1,100	1,112
0.025	304	576	816	1,024	1,200	1,344	1,456	1,536	1,584	1,600
0.020	475	900	1,275	1,600	1,875	2,100	2,275	2,400	2,475	2,500
0.015	845	1,600	2,267	2,845	3,334	3,734	4,045	4,267	4,400	4,445
0.010	1,900	3,600	5,100	6,400	7,500	8,400	9,100	9,600	9,900	10,000
0.005	7,600	14,400	20,400	25,600	30,000	33,600	36,400	38,400	39,600	40,000

*The numbers in the table are the sample sizes required to compute a 95.5 percent confidence interval that is plus or minus h percent around the estimated percentage p.

width of plus or minus 5 percent? For a 95.5 percent confidence interval z is 2. With $z=2$, $p=.7$, and $h=0.05$, the above equation recommends a sample size of $N=336$ observations.

CASE STUDY

National Computer Systems, Inc.

COMPANY BACKGROUND

National Computer Systems, Inc., a $300 million dollar company, headquartered in Eden Prairie, Minnesota, is a leader in the field of forms-based information collection systems for education, business, and banking. Some of the company's major products are optical mark reading (OMR) scanners, software, and forms used in schools and standardized exams. These are the familiar forms with the bubbles to be filled in with the number 2 pencil.

THE FIELD SERVICE DIVISION

NCS's Field Service Division is headquartered in Eagan, Minnesota, and has about 425 employees including approximately 200 technicians. With 99 service locations, NCS technicians can reach 98 percent of the continental United States within two hours. The Field Service Division supports both NCS proprietary hardware and third-party hardware under agreements with other original equipment manufacturers. NCS provides third-party service for equipment such as minicomputers, super-minicomputers, microcomputers, graphics workstations, and computer peripherals.

SERVICE CALL MANAGEMENT SYSTEM

All service calls are received in Eagan, Minnesota, by a group of 14 dispatchers. When a service call is received, it is entered into the FIELDWATCH system, and the customer is told that "someone from NCS will get back to you within one hour." Based on the product type, either the service call is routed to the Technical Assistance Center (TAC) or the primary technician assigned to the machine is paged. If a technician is paged, the page goes out within three minutes. The technician has 30 minutes to call a dispatcher and to commit to the service call. If the technician has not committed to the service call within 30 minutes, a second page is sent and the area manager is paged. If a technician still does not commit to the service call within another 15 minutes, the regional manager is paged. If one hour passes without a technician having committed to the service call, the service call is escalated up to the vice president of operations. The system maintains technician status information so that if a technician is sick, on vacation, or in training, the secondary technician is paged instead of the primary technician.

In the phone conversation with the dispatcher, the technician reports his or her whereabouts, receives information for the call (or calls) assigned, commits to the service call, and sets an ETA (estimated time of arrival) for the service call. The technician then immediately calls the customers and arranges visits. The FIELDWATCH system will produce an exception report if the technician does not then meet the ETA commitment within certain tolerances. Technicians clear (close) calls via a voice box (recording). They have both an "expert line" and a "prompted line." The prompted line prompts the technician for each data item, whereas the expert line requires that the technicians know the correct order for the data items. Dispatchers access the voice box to enter this information whenever they have the time to do so.

Area managers manage the technician's service calls via personal computers and modems that communicate to the division headquarters in Eagan. Area managers use their computers both to get information on new service calls and to update service calls. The only information that is communicated by means of person-to-person phone conversations is the delivery of the service call to the technician assigned. From that point on, service call update through service call closure can happen by use of remote personal computers or voice mail.

Some larger customers manage their own service calls via access to the service call management screen. This saves the customer time, provides more information, and saves money for NCS. NCS has found this to be a good selling point for their services.

The performance of the system at NCS has been excellent with about 96 percent of all service calls receiving a commitment from a technician within one hour. The average response time is about two hours with very few service calls having a response time of greater than four hours.

PERFORMANCE MEASUREMENT FOR TECHNICIANS

NCS's management measures field service performance with the following variables:

First Time Effectiveness.   This is the percentage of service calls that are repaired the first time a technician is sent to the site. Service calls may not be completed the first time due to lack of parts, or because the customer would not allow the technician into the building, the customer was not available, or it was the end of the workday.

PM Percent Complete.   Each month each technician is given a list of PM (preventive maintenance) jobs that need to be completed for the month. NCS's new standard for technicians is 100 percent completion.

Response Time by Contract Type.   Response time is defined as the elapsed time from the service call open event to the arrival time on the customer's site. This report displays a frequency distribution of response times by contract types. Table 1 is a simplified version of the report. NCS's goal is to have an average response time that is less than four hours.

Time to Commit to Service Calls.   This is defined as the elapsed time from the service call open event to the time the technician makes the commitment to take the service call. This time is also displayed as a distribution.

TABLE 1
Response Time Report (Simplified)

Technician 213
Contract Type 1

Response time frequency

1 hour	2 hours	3 hours	4 hours	5 hours	6 hours
45	57	21	4	2	1

Downtime per Service Call.   This is the sum of the response time and the repair time (including the time to wait for parts).

The Number of Repeat Service Calls.   This is the number of times that technicians have to return to a customer's site to repair the same machine within a specified number of days. This report is given to senior management, but is not distributed to the field.

Customer Surveys.   The customer survey at NCS is increasing in importance as a means of evaluating total system performance as well as individual technician performance. Historically, NCS mailed "scanable" surveys to about one-twelfth of their customer base on a monthly basis. The new policy is to randomly select 50 calls per day that have had a service call in the prior three days. Each day a dispatcher is assigned to call these 50 customers, collect the survey information, and interactively enter this information on the survey database using custom-designed interactive computer screens. This method is better than a mail survey for several reasons:

1. The dispatchers are calling the individual who is the "end-user" rather than the person who requested the service. These may not be the same people. Many companies have service calls reported by some centrally controlled office.
2. The dispatchers capture the results of the phone survey on-line.
3. This system has a higher response rate than the mail survey.
4. The phone survey is more timely than a mail survey. People forget very quickly. The three-day delay is a very short delay compared to most mail surveys.

The key question on the survey deals with customer satisfaction. The vast majority of customers report that they are very satisfied with NCS's service. If a customer is only "satisfied," the service call information is given to the area manager to see if they can improve next time. If a customer is dissatisfied, the information is given to the area manager and to the regional manager. If a customer is extremely dissatisfied, the regional manager must call the customer back and find out what happened and try to recover.

PERFORMANCE MEASUREMENT FOR DISPATCHERS

Many companies use phone statistics such as the average time on the phone with a customer to measure dispatcher performance. This information is easy to obtain from the ACD (automatic call distribution system) and is therefore very tempting to use for performance measurement. NCS is very careful in the use of these phone statistics. The goal is to help the customer, not to minimize the amount of time that is spent on the phone with the customer. Average talk time is not used as a performance measure for dispatchers. Phone statistics are used only to measure dispatchers as a departmental team on the basis of call hold time and abandoned service calls.

Dispatchers deal with both customers and technicians. Being both providers and consumers of the service call information, they are highly motivated to maintain high standards of data accuracy.

CHALLENGES

Like many other providers of third-party service, NCS faces many challenges in the third-party business as machines become more reliable, hardware prices (and service contract prices) continue to fall, and competition becomes more price-sensitive. Minimizing parts inventories is always a big problem for all field service organizations—especially for those in the third-party business.

Invoicing issues are also common complaints for providers of field service. NCS management is in the process of improving its invoicing procedures so that it can produce more timely and accurate invoices for both time and materials service calls and service calls covered under a service agreement.

Field service staffing issues are extremely complex. The process of determining the right number of technicians for a service location requires information on the machine population, failure rates, machine density, travel times, and many other factors. This process must be based on having accurate information from the technicians.

KEY POINTS

NCS is doing an excellent job of managing both customer expectations and service delivery. NCS commits up front to the customer—"you should expect to hear from somebody at NCS within one hour"—and they deliver on this promise. Technicians usually call the customer back in less than an hour and establish an estimated time of arrival. This makes the customer feel that NCS is providing almost immediate attention from their own personal technician. The system of primary technicians gives both the technician and the customer a sense of ownership in the relationship.

The company is using information technology such as FIELDWATCH, the online customer survey, and other systems for competitive advantage. Computer-based systems are available to technicians, area managers, and even some key customers.

The customer survey at NCS is simple but very effective at assessing customer satisfaction. The phone survey technique ensures timely and accurate information from the right person. Follow-up management demonstrates a high level of commitment to service quality.

ACKNOWLEDGEMENTS

The author thanks Ms. Barb Schmit, Manager of Information Systems at NCS, for her help in preparing this case.

CHAPTER 5

SERVICE CALL MANAGEMENT: MANAGING THE CUSTOMER INTERFACE

INTRODUCTION

The service call is the basic field service transaction. The arrival of a service call (service request, service order) from a customer (consumer, end-user) is the event that drives the field service organization. Whereas manufacturing has production orders, field service has service calls. The difference is in the timing—field service organizations typically measure response times in hours or minutes rather than days or weeks.

Managing the service call is essentially managing the customer interface. The service call must be handled very carefully and very professionally. This chapter deals with a wide range of issues regarding service call management including:

- Service call management. What is a service call and how is it managed?
- Service call data entry. What steps are necessary to enter a service call into the service call management system?
- Service call assignment. How are service calls assigned to technicans?
- Service call escalation. How should service calls be monitored so that management's attention is directed to problems at the appropriate times?
- Service call clearing. What data should be collected on a service call when it is completed and how should this data be collected?
- Service cycle time reduction. How can nonvalue added times be removed from response time and downtime?

- Dispatcher staffing. How many dispatchers should be available during each period of the day?
- Centralization of dispatching. How should dispatching centers be set up? Should the service organization have only one, centralized dispatching center or many regional centers?
- Technical assistance center. How can a technical assistance center be used best to help customers and technicians in the field?
- Software support. How do we support our software in the field?

SERVICE CALL MANAGEMENT

Service organizations deal with a variety of types of service calls. These include:

Emergency Maintenance (EM)
An EM call is a response to an urgent request for on-site repair of a failed machine. Much of field service management is designed to handle this type of service call. Some organizations make a distinction between major problems (hard-down) and minor problems (soft-down). A hard-down is a machine that is totally out of service, whereas a soft-down is a machine that is crippled but is able to still provide some service.

Preventive Maintenance (PM)
A PM is a service call that provides preventive maintenance such as cleaning, replacing parts that wear out quickly, and checking the machine. PMs are usually performed on a regular basis (as determined by the manufacturer or the contract) rather than on an emergency basis. PMs are generally assigned to technicians to be done sometime during the month or are scheduled in advance. However, preventive maintenance is often done in conjunction with an emergency maintenance repair just because it is more convenient to do so. Response time is not an issue for PMs. Some field service organizations schedule PMs simply to maintain a presence at the customer's account.

A special type of preventive maintenance called *predictive maintenance* is discussed in the chapter on advanced technologies. The predictive maintenance is simply preventive maintenance that is scheduled in response to some indication that the machine may be about to fail.

Installations

This is the setting up of a newly purchased (or leased) machine and may involve substantial amounts of construction, testing, integration, and training effort. (For example, Honeywell Commercial Buildings Group often requires many weeks to install a control system for a heating/cooling unit.) Installations are often scheduled and, therefore, are somewhat easier to manage than emergency maintenance calls.

De-installations

A de-installation is the removal of a machine from a site and is a scheduled activity similar to that of an installation.

Customer Training

Some companies create a service call when a technician is required to provide customers with on-site training in how to use a machine.

Figure 5–1 presents the time line of the process flow for a typical emergency maintenance service call. Many service organizations will deviate from this slightly. The flow is described in detail below:

FIGURE 5–1
Time Line for "Commit" Time for Emergency Maintenance

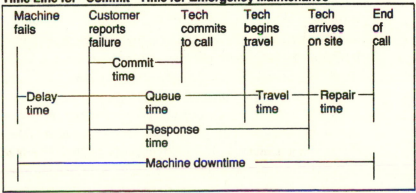

1. The customer's machine fails.

2. The customer detects the failure. A delay may occur here until the customer discovers the problem.

3. A phone call is made to the service provider to report the failure. The end-user/operator or an administrator in the end-user's organization (e.g., purchasing or contract administration) calls the dispatcher to report the machine failure. No delay is experienced if the machine has self-diagnostic equipment that automatically signals a problem to the operator and/or places a call to the service provider. For some large customer organizations, some service providers provide computer access so that the customer can enter the service call directly to the call management system without having to talk to a dispatcher. This option can potentially reduce hold time, improve information accuracy, and reduce response time.

4. The dispatcher answers the phone. Ideally, the dispatcher (call-taker) answers the phone call with a very short hold time for the customer. The telephone number should cause the ACD (automatic call distribution) system to direct the call to the appropriate dispatcher who handles that type of service call.

5. Customer identification (model, serial, etc.). The dispatcher asks the caller for some identification. Ideally, the caller will have the model and serial numbers for the machine readily available. However, the call management system must have the capability to search the database by the company name, phone number, or other fields. The level of aggregation is a difficult problem here. A system is a collection of components that all have model/serial numbers which in turn may have subcomponents which may also have model and serial numbers. Some companies are experimenting with the "ANI" technology which allows the phone system to automatically identify the customer's phone number from data that is sent along with the phone call. This information allows the service organization to quickly identify a customer, route the call to the appropriate dispatcher, and display the information on the dispatcher's screen—even before the customer has

begun the conversation. The disadvantage of this technology is that many customers are calling from large organizations with only one ANI number.

6. Attempt to avoid the service call. It is desirable to try to avoid the service call by referring the call to a Technical Assistance Center (TAC) or by having the dispatcher apply some tools (such as a simple list of questions, a simple question tree, or an AI system) in an attempt to resolve the problem over the phone. In some organizations, this is done after it is verified that the customer has a service agreement (the next step).

7. Verify the service arrangement. Ideally, the service call management system will be able to confirm (or disconfirm) that the machine is covered by a warranty or a service agreement. This is often a difficult issue because contracts can be written for companies, sites, systems (machines working together), machines, or major components of machines. Some companies have a policy that the customer should be given the benefit of the doubt and allow the contract verification to be done after the customer has hung up, or after the technician has serviced the machine. If it is a "time and materials" (T&M) call, some service providers require a purchase order number from the customer before service can be provided.

8. Verify site information. After determining that a site visit is required, it is important to verify certain information about the site visit such as the name and phone number of the person to contact, the acceptable time window for repair, etc.

9. Assign a technician to the service call. The service call should be assigned to a technician either when the call is received (the account representative policy) or when a technician calls the dispatcher to request more work.

10. Technician calls the customer. In order to provide phone consultation, assess the severity of the problem, and, if needed, schedule a site visit, the technician calls the customer. If a site visit is needed, the technician establishes a sense of priority and a feasible time window and then estimates a time of arrival. Empowering technicians to schedule their own work

is a good idea, especially when dispatching is centralized and the dispatchers do not have good estimates for travel times. For some service businesses, it is important to know when a product kit will be available before making an estimate of the time of arrival.

11. Travel to the customer site. Travel times often take about as long as repair times. For some large military contractors and other manufacturers, a significant amount of the time in getting to the customer site is spent passing through security and finding the machine. This is a particularly difficult process if the technician has to carry heavy testing equipment and must walk through several buildings.

12. Diagnose and repair the problem. Diagnosing the problem is often the largest segment of the time spent on site. This step may also involve some direct customer contact for training and/or explaining the problem to the user.

13. Clear the call. Clearing (or closing) the call involves capturing the data necessary for billing, performance measurement, capacity planning, sales, feedback for product design, etc.

The following sections will explore some of the management issues related to this process.

SERVICE CALL DATA ENTRY

As soon as a customer finds that a machine has failed (which may be some time after it actually has failed), the customer calls the service provider to request service. Many service organizations provide a toll-free phone number for this purpose. Sometimes the equipment operator will report the failure; however, in some organizations, the user will communicate the problem to another internal organization (such as a central maintenance organization) which has formal procedures for processing the service request.

The dispatcher receives the phone call and enters it into a computer system. Ideally, the system allows the dispatcher to very quickly identify the customer and the model without having to rekey any basic information such as the customer's name, address, phone number, contact, billing address, and so forth. After the customer has been identified, the dispatcher will determine if the model is covered by a warranty or service agreement. If it is not, the dispatcher must determine how the customer intends to pay for the service. Some service companies require purchase order numbers for time and materials calls expected to exceed a specified amount.

After the service agreement/invoicing issues have been settled, the dispatcher determines the type of machine problem. The dispatcher may then attempt to help the customer fix the machine or may route the service call to a technical assistance center (TAC). If the dispatcher and the TAC technician are unable to resolve the problem remotely, the call is assigned to a technician.

Some field service management software assists in assigning priorities to service calls. One way this is done is by defining separate factors for importance and urgency. Importance is a characteristic of the account, customer, and contract, while urgency is a characteristic of the specific service call. The importance and urgency factors can interact to define some sort of service call priority index. One way to implement this is to define a response time target table that is a function of the model, importance, and urgency. This table is referenced every time a service call is added to the system. The response time target then drives the priorities for technicians. (This is somewhat analogous to using due dates to drive the priorities in the job shop manufacturing environment where the due dates are set based on the importance of the customer and the urgency of the job.)

SERVICE CALL ASSIGNMENT

An interesting article in *Good Housekeeping* discusses the problem of customers "thinking that the company keeps technicians hanging on pegs in a large inventory." Commenting on the problem of finding a good system for scheduling these technicians, the article states, "Whoever comes up with *that* deserves the Nobel Peace Prize."

Many service organizations employ an account representative or primary technician policy for assigning technicians. With this policy, area managers assign a primary technician to each account (or machine or system). They also may assign a secondary and a tertiary technician. Normally the service call is assigned to the primary technician (the account representative). If the primary technician is not on duty or cannot handle it in a reasonable time frame, the service call is passed to the secondary technician. If no one can handle the service call within specified time limits, the service call is passed back to the area manager, who may call the customer and/or find another technician to handle it. The advantage of the primary technician policy is that the primary technician has a sense of ownership of the account, gains detailed knowledge of the customer's machines, systems, buildings, and people, and builds a relationship with the customer that is helpful when selling supplies, new machines, and service agreement renewals.

An alternative approach commonly found in the field service industry is to assign the closest available trained technician. This approach requires that the dispatcher have a good idea of the geography, travel times, technician training, distribution of repair times, and other information about technician availability. The advantage of this approach is better than average travel times and response times. The disadvantage is that the technicians may not develop a very close relationship with the customers because they do not see them as regularly. Also, the technicians may not feel responsible for the customers since they have no sense of ownership for the accounts.

Some organizations differentiate between different levels of training. A newly trained technician might be assigned to a service call in order to develop some proficiency. Conversely, a highly trained technician might be assigned because the mean (or the variance) of the repair time for that technician is the lowest or because the machine is a particularly difficult one to repair.

SERVICE CALL ESCALATION

Call escalation is an extremely important aspect of service call management, particularly for emergency calls. The majority of service calls are completed in a reasonable amount of time and the customer is satisfied with the service. Pareto's Law (the "80-20" rule) suggests that this is true for about 80 percent of the calls. However, for a small percentage of calls (about 20 percent), the response time may be longer when a technician is sick, in training, on vacation, stuck on a long repair, etc. When these problems occur, it is very important for the field service organization to have an early warning system to signal that a service failure is about to occur. This concept is called "exception" reporting in the management information field. Management must manage the tail of the response time distribution. It is the customer with a very long response time who will be angry, tell many other people about the poor service, and not purchase additional service agreements, hardware, or supplies.

A service call is "escalated" to a higher level of control when some aspect of the call does not meet a management-defined threshold parameter. These standards may be defined in at least four ways:

1. The technician did not call the customer within the standard "technician telephone response time" allowed after the service call was received.
2. The response time for the call was longer than the standard for this customer or this type of machine.
3. The repair time for the machine did not meet the standard repair time for this type of machine.
4. The completion time for the call did not meet the standard.

Management can control the number of exception reports generated by controlling the standards and by designing the system so that the appropriate people receive the reports in a timely manner.

Some of the commercial field service management software allow the user to set these standards based on the importance of the customer (or customer's contract or customer's machine) and the urgency of the call. For example, if the customer is very important and the call is quite urgent, the escalation parameters might be set to 15 minutes to call the customer back and one hour for response time. These systems allow the user to set up parameter tables based on importance and urgency codes.

SERVICE CALL CLEARING

Upon completion of a service call, data needs to be collected from the technician. This process is called "clearing" or "closing" the call. The kinds of data items that are required include:

- Service history for the machine: This is used to help technicians identify longer-term trends and to keep the product configurations up to date.
- Time and materials information: This is used for billing purposes if the service call was not covered by warranty or a service agreement.
- Service parts inventory usage information: This is useful for maintaining perpetual inventory records for the technician's vehicle. Many companies will use this information to automatically replenish the technician's vehicle. It is also important for billing and for auditing technicians (theft of parts can be a problem).
- Problem analysis: This information is used to feed a Pareto analysis for product improvement

SERVICE CYCLE TIME REDUCTION

The "just-in-time" (JIT) revolution has had a major impact on reducing cycle times for manufacturing firms in both the United States and Europe. As manufacturing lead times have been compressed, quality has improved, costs have gone down, customer lead times have been compressed, and customer satisfaction has increased. The basic JIT ideas can also be applied in improving service call cycle times (reduce both response time and downtime). Specifically, the following JIT concepts can be applied to reduce service call cycle time:

- Eliminate "nonvalue added activities" where possible. For example, having a technician drive back to a branch office in order to wait for the next service call does not add value to the customer. The "litmus test" questions here are, "Does this add value to the customer?" and, "Does the customer care if we do this or not?" If the activity does not add value to the customer and the customer does not care, then attempt to eliminate the activity if possible.
- Identify the queues and attempt to reduce the waiting times. Find where the significant queues (waiting times) are. Although

the longest waiting time nearly always involves waiting for a technician to become available, time spent waiting for a dispatcher, printer, telephone, parts, or computer may also be significant. These should be reduced as much as possible. Dispatcher call hold-times for both technicians and customers can be reduced by means of flexible dispatcher staffing so that the dispatcher capacity better matches call demand patterns.

- Eliminate multiple handling of the same service call. The process should be made as seamless as possible. For example, one company has a group of dispatchers who log service calls from customers. The dispatchers then pass the service calls on to another group of dispatchers who assign the service calls to technicians. By the time a service call gets to a technician, some information has been lost and the customer has already been waiting for some time.

- Eliminate wasted motion. Encourage technicians to learn to manage their diagnosis and repair efficiently. They should have the right tools available and should organize their repair activities so that time is not wasted in traveling to/from the vehicle or looking for the correct tool.

- Encourage workers to be multifunctional. Training technicians to handle multiple models is a wide-spread practice. The question here is, "How many models and how much inventory can a technician handle?" In manufacturing, it has been found that the traditional approach of having a few skills for each worker is not a good idea. The same is probably true for field service. As artificial intelligence tools proliferate and as TAC groups become more sophisticated in helping technicians in the field, it is likely that technicians will be certified to repair a wider variety of models.

- Break down functional silos. Functional silos are the barriers that most companies have between the functional areas (e.g., marketing, sales, engineering, field service, etc.). The principle here is that these silos inhibit performance and should be broken down. IBM's new field service strategy seems to be addressing some of these issues.

- Simplify the process. A simple, transparent process is easier for all to understand and is much more likely to be perceived as fair by everyone involved.

DISPATCHER STAFFING

The term "dispatcher" has several different meanings. There are at least three different types of dispatcher jobs commonly used in field service organizations.

1. *Call takers*. These people deal only with customers. They take customer phone calls, enter and verify service call information, and sometimes attempt to fix the machines remotely. Call takers do not do any dispatching and, therefore, should not be considered dispatchers.

2. *Technician-assignment dispatchers*. These dispatchers deal only with technicians. They are often heavily involved in assigning calls, communicating call information, receiving parts orders, clearing calls, etc.

3. *Dual-purpose dispatchers*. These are dispatchers who do both of the above.

The argument against the dual-purpose dispatcher is that the job requires many different skills—dealing with customers, fixing machines remotely, assigning/scheduling technicians, and so forth. The advantage of this combined position is that the enlarged job description gives the dispatcher a better understanding of the total process, and, therefore, improves performance quality. A secondary advantage is better labor productivity because the dispatcher's workload is more evenly spread between the two jobs during the workday.

CENTRALIZATION OF DISPATCHING

Maintaining centralized versus regional (or local) dispatching centers is a controversial issue. The advantages of centralized dispatching include:

Higher dispatcher productivity occurs because the time-of-day fluctuations of incoming call rates tend to even out when dispatchers are working with multiple time zones.

The larger call rate for the pooled system will have a lower coefficient of variation (standard deviation divided by the mean) and will, therefore, tend to have less dispatcher idle time and lower hold time. (This can be proven statistically with some reasonable assumptions.)

A centralized system means less duplication of communication and information systems.

Centralized systems making training and communication easier. It is also easier to implement an AI system in one location rather than in several.

Advantages of regional (decentralized) dispatching include:

Customers and technicians have a sense of local ownership and control over the dispatching process.

Dispatchers have a good understanding of the local geography and customer base so they are less likely to send technicians on unreasonably long trips.

When billing is done locally, it can be more easily coordinated with local dispatching.

The trend appears to be toward centralization of dispatching. (Note: this centralization trend is also apparent in other functions such as TAC, depot repair, and service parts inventory.)

TECHNICAL ASSISTANCE CENTER

A technical assistance center (TAC) is typically staffed by well-trained technicians who often assist customers with problems using telecommunications or computer technology, help other technicians with difficult repairs, or both. The advantages of remote repair are very significant. The customer experiences shorter downtime, and both technician and vehicle costs are lower. This concept is often referred to in the operations management literature as "getting the customer involved in producing the product." Obviously, this can be a win–win project for both the service provider and the customer.

On the negative side, however, customers sometimes feel that the service organization does not care very much, if the service organization is constantly trying to avoid sending a technician. This is especially true if the TAC people are consistently unable to repair a machine remotely.

Some customers simply do not want to be bothered with the hassle of trying to fix the machine themselves. They reason that "We paid for on-site service, so just send the technician." In these situations, it is often better to just send the technician.

Basic tools for TAC technicians include a complete set of documentation, tools for remote diagnosis, and possibly some artificial intelligence software for diagnosis and repair (discussed in the chapter on advanced technologies). The software support should allow TAC technicians to quickly identify and document problems and fixes so that the organization can learn from its experience. Communication equipment (pagers, voice boxes, etc.) to facilitate communication between TAC and the field is also crucial.

Some technicians criticize TAC groups as out of touch with the real problems in the field. By involving TAC technicians in the training of field technicians, and by rotating field technicians through TAC group assignments on a regular basis, this issue can be addressed.

SOFTWARE SUPPORT

Many field service organizations today find themselves providing increasing "help-desk" support for software in the field. Software support has many similarities to field service support in that it requires attention to model/serial numbers (software version), customer perceptions of service, response times, and so on. The most significant differences are that software support can usually be done completely from remote locations and usually involves consulting rather than repair. Typically, a software consultant sits at a computer and discusses the problem with the customer over the telephone—ideally with the same release of the software. It is often possible for the consultant to remotely view and even control the customer's computer screen. Software fixes are often express mailed to the customer; however, it is usually possible for updated software to be communicated electronically (via modem) to the user's machine.

Software support people are basically "software technicians." Performance measurement for the software support group is very similar to that for technicians—response times, repair times, repair quality, customer satisfaction, etc. Major differences between software support people and technicians include:

- Software support people rarely have to leave the help-desk to provide support. They can generally provide diagnosis and fixes over the phone lines.
- Software support people are often more involved in training and implementation issues, which tend to be "softer" issues and, therefore, more difficult to evaluate.
- Software support people are often closer to the engineering (product design) function as they communicate software bugs and other problems. (Technicians *should* also be close to engineering for product design issues.)

Once a fix is found for a problem, the software consultants need to document what they have done so that others can benefit. The software support staff should be consulted on the design for new software in much the same way that technicians are consulted on product design.

CONCLUSIONS

Service calls are the basic element of field service management systems. Managing the service call is truly managing the customer interaction and must be done very carefully in order to ensure customer satisfaction.

The key principle in this chapter is that service call handling is a process that must be carefully studied from the customer's point of view. Service recovery and exception reporting (call escalation) should be carefully designed into this process design. Many steps of the process can be improved by the introduction of technologies such as computer systems, communications systems, and artificial intelligence/ expert systems.

The service call management must system interface to the accounting system (for billing and accounts receivable), to contract management (for contract validation), to human resources management systems (for training information), to engineering (for product design feedback), and to manufacturing (for quality improvement feedback). Nearly all of these interfaces rely on computer-based information system technologies. Many of these interface issues are considered further in the chapters on Service Management Information Systems and on Inter-functional connections.

CASE STUDY

Norstan Communications Inc.

COMPANY BACKGROUND

Norstan is a rapidly growing $135 million company headquartered in Maple Grove, Minnesota. The company's business is primarily the sale, installation, and servicing of private telecommunications systems under distributor agreements with ROLM and other telecommunications equipment manufacturers. Norstan's strategy is "to become a one-stop shopping resource for all of its customers' communications needs." Customer service and support play a critical role in this strategy.

THE FIELD SERVICE DIVISION

Norstan is organized into three regions. The Central Region (Maple Grove, Minnesota), the Eastern Region (Cleveland, Ohio), and the Southwestern Region (Phoenix, Arizona). The Central Region employs about 160 technicians, 14 dispatchers, 4 technicians in the Technical Assistance Center (TAC) group, and 6 engineers/product specialists.

TECHNICAL ASSISTANCE CENTER

When a service call is received at the regional service center, the dispatcher makes a judgment about whether it might be a candidate for a remote repair. If it is, a message is sent via the FIELDWATCH system to the Technical Assistance Center (TAC). The TAC technicians have a screen that prioritizes these calls. After completing a service order, they take the next service order in priority, and attempt to diagnose and repair the system remotely. If they cannot repair the equipment remotely, they page the primary technician for the service call, who is sent to the customer site.

A group of product specialist engineers sit nearby and serve as consultants to the technicians who work in the TAC group. This arrangement allows for a good flow of information both ways.

SERVICE COMMITMENTS

About 95 percent of Norstan customers have service contracts. Nearly all of these contracts explicitly state a response time commitment between 90 minutes to 4 hours for major repairs. For minor repairs the response time commitment is much longer. Norstan uses the Response Time Report to help its sales people determine the appropriate response time commitment to use for service contracts (both for renewals and for new contracts). For example a "3 by 24" contract makes a 3-hour commitment for a major problem and a 24-hour response time commitment for a minor problem. A problem is considered to be a major problem if 20 percent or more of the network is down or if the system is considered to be a critical system such as a medical system or an ACD (Automatic Call Distribution system). A "system down" condition is especially serious. In extreme cases, Norstan will help a customer out by supplying UPS (Universal Power System) so that their phone systems can continue to work even without local power.

The call escalation system alerts the dispatcher when a call is approaching the response time commitment.

PROACTIVE DIAGNOSTICS

On a nightly basis Norstan polls customers' switchers via remote telephone communications and personal computer technologies. A computer at Norstan polls customers' systems remotely and accesses the error tables. If any problems are detected, the information is sent to the dispatch center. A technican looks at this information and handles the problem remotely or generates a repair ticket for a service call. This is done every night between midnight and 6:00 A.M.

Most of Norstan's customers also have an ''alarm dialer'' that will send a message to the dispatch center with a display code. The display code identifies the customer and the type of problem.

With these proactive systems, Norstan sometimes knows about the problem before the customer finds out about it.

CHALLENGES

The constant callenge at Norstan (and most other service organizations) is to find ways to offer improved service without increasing costs. There is also a need to be sure that other functional areas understand that service is more than a necessary evil—service is a product like many other products that the company offers.

KEY POINTS

In interviews with Norstan management, the word ''proactive'' came up several times. The company is committed to preventing serious problems rather than waiting until they occur.

The Technical Assistance Center is really just a group of remote technicians who can diagnose and repair machines at a distance. This concept is here today with telecommunications equipment and is quickly becoming a reality for many other types of equipment.

ACKNOWLEDGEMENTS

The author wishes to thank Mr. Craig Kalscheur, Mr. Phil Dismuke, and Mr. Rich Scorza of Norstan for their help in writing this case.

CHAPTER 6

SERVICE PARTS INVENTORY MANAGEMENT: MANAGING THE INVENTORY INVESTMENT

INTRODUCTION

Service parts inventory management is a big business. Inventories of service parts in the United States exceed $100 billion. The U.S. Defense budget alone includes tens of billions of dollars for service parts. Yet, half the parts in many service parts inventories have not moved in two years. With relatively short life cycles and highly variable demand, the annual carrying and obsolescence cost for service parts in the United States is in the billions of dollars.

Most service parts managers agree that too many service calls are not completed the first time because the right parts were not available when needed. Customers may wait a few hours for a technician to arrive but they will have to wait days if the right parts are not readily available. Express mail services, such as Federal Express, have built their businesses to a large degree on sending parts to distraught customers.

With high inventory investment and high service level requirements, service parts inventories often provide an opportunity to make dramatic improvements in both service quality and productivity. Organizations can use information and good management practices to simultaneously reduce inventories and increase customer service levels.

Managing service parts is different from managing raw materials or distribution inventories in many ways. Service parts inventory managers are confronted with problems such as:

- Warranties from parts suppliers.
- Warranties for customers.
- Parts moving out to the field and back to be repaired or disposed.

- Repairable inventories.
- Recyclable parts.
- Inventories in vehicles.
- Highly uncertain replenishment lead times.
- Short life cycles for many items.
- Initial provisioning.
- Final buy decisions.
- Many parts with low demand.
- High parts cost, high margins, and high stockout cost.

The fundamentals of inventory and logistics management principles can be found in the book by Vollmann, Berry, and Whybark. This chapter extends these principles to issues unique to service parts management. Specifically, this chapter will address the following issues:

Field service logistics network.

Service parts purchasing management.

Service parts warehouse inventory management.

Service parts logistics inventory management.

Repairable inventory management.

Pricing service parts.

FIELD SERVICE LOGISTICS NETWORK

Before suggesting specific management practices for managing field service inventories, it is important to briefly describe the field service logistics network. Service parts businesses have a wide range of customers including dealers, field service organizations, international field service organizations, and end-user customers. Each customer has a unique set of requirements for service levels, lead times, and prices.

These customers can be served from a number of different service parts inventories stocking locations including:

Central warehouse.

Regional warehouses.

Local parts depots (sometimes called parts "pods").

Lock boxes (often found in bus depots).

Technician vehicles.

Customer locations.

A central warehouse has the advantage of not duplicating safety stock inventories; however, a central warehouse does not store inventory close to the technicians or customers in the field. Many firms have regional and local warehouses in order to reduce lead times to the field. These warehouses require significantly more inventory but may provide better service levels.

Lock boxes allow the organization to keep a small inventory of expensive parts in one location so that several technicians do not have to carry the parts. If a part is kept in the technician's vehicle, the customer gets nearly instantaneous service; however, it is difficult to determine how many parts should be stored in the vehicle in order to find the best tradeoff between service levels and inventory investment. Vehicle size also imposes a limit on how much can be carried with the technician. Technician vehicle inventory issues will be discussed in more detail later in this chapter.

Some customers maintain their own inventories. The APICS proceedings on ''MRO'' (maintenance and repair operations) contain information on managing these types of inventories. This problem is similar to the ''car-stock'' problem that will be discussed later in this chapter.

Inventory stocking decisions are influenced by the length of the lead time requirements, product life, demand rate for the parts, and transportation costs. Some organizations are finding that the cost of having regional and local inventories outweighs the cost of sending parts by commercial overnight delivery via Federal Express or some other express mail carrier. Most stocking locations must have some safety stock. Multiple stocking locations tend to have much more inventory than a single central location. Total warehouse inventory tends to increase with the square root of the number of warehouses. For example, if the number of warehouses increases by a factor of 2, the inventory investment will increase roughly by a factor of $\sqrt{2} = 1.414$. Looking at it from the opposite perspective, reducing the number of warehouses can make a substantial reduction in the total inventory investment required to support the field.

Field service parts management involves sending good parts and consumables out to the field (in order to replenish regional warehouses, vehicle stocks, customer demands, etc.), properly disposing of bad parts, sending repairable parts back to be repaired, and returning warranty parts to the vendor. Inventory records for each stocking location should at least keep track of both good and bad parts in inventory. The service parts information system should provide clear directions on how to dispose of each part. Ideally, this information is on a computer, readily available to the technician, and easily changeable by the central service parts management. The justification for this last point is that the company might want to temporarily call in a sample of some parts in order to study a particular problem.

SERVICE PARTS PURCHASING MANAGEMENT

Service parts purchasing management has much in common with purchasing for a manufacturing or distribution firm. The book by Joseph Carter presents a good description of purchasing management principles. This section discusses the following topics:

- Service parts purchasing system design principles.
- Forecasting service parts demand.
- Demand filter.
- Tracking signal.
- Reorder points and safety stocks.
- Purchase order quantities.
- First and last lot buys.

Service Parts Purchasing System Design Principles

The following is a list of design principles that should be the foundation of any service parts purchasing/inventory planning system:

Principle 1. The System Should Be Designed with a Long-Term Strategic Perspective.   A purchasing/inventory planning system plays a critical role in the ability to compete in the marketplace. The system should be designed with a long-term strategic view that considers trade-offs between cost, service, flexibility, and quality.

Principle 2. The System Should Be Flexible.   As the business changes over time, the system requirements will change. In order to be flexible, the system needs to be transparent to the users so that they are the master and the system is the servant. To accomplish this goal, the system's logic must be clear so that the users can understand its operation and override it where appropriate.

Principle 3. The System Should Be Error Resistant.   The system should warn the user of potential data entry errors, serious decisions, and so on. For example, the system should never allow the user to enter an erroneous stock number. The system might also ask the user to double check a quantity if it is beyond a certain reasonable tolerance.

Principle 4. The System Should Be Well-Documented and the Documentation Should Be Readily Available.   The ideal documentation is online and context-sensitive. "Context-sensitive" means that the user can hit a help key in the context of a screen, or even a field on a screen, and receive help on that screen and/or field. A key feature of this documentation is the data dictionary. It is best if the terms used internally by the company are consistent with industry use. (This makes it easier to use standard reference materials and also makes training easier.)

Principle 5. The System Should Allow the Users to Get the Job Done Efficiently.   Many simple but powerful features are needed to assist the users in doing their jobs efficiently and effectively. Some specific ideas include:

- Finding records/entering stock numbers. Users should never have to type in a complete stock number, order number, etc. They should be able to scroll through a list with the arrow keys and/or type the first few characters and have the system do a search. Similarly, once an item number has been found, the user should be able to move to all screens related to that item without having to re-enter the stock number.

- Exception notices/prioritization of effort. When a user is working on expediting, releasing orders, etc., records should be prioritized so that the more important work is done first. Exception reports highlight the most important information for immediate attention.
- Avoidance of codes on the screen. Overuse of codes can lead to confusion, poor training, etc. It is often better to avoid cryptic codes (particularly nonmeaningful ones such as the asterisk) and use more room on the screen to print more meaningful information. This may mean that multiple screens and/or windows are needed for some functions. As long as it is easy to switch between screens or move between windows, this should not be a significant problem.

Principle 6. Graphical Display Should Be Used where Appropriate. Time series data (e.g., sales history) can often be best understood with a simple graph. Even a character-based graph (rather than a bit-mapped graph) can help the inventory analyst to better understand the data. Simple graphs are also very useful for displaying distributions of backorders and the like.

Principle 7. The System Should Be Supported by a Formal Education and Training Program for the Users. Due to the normal changes in personnel over time, a formal approach to an ongoing education and training program is very important for the success of the system. One method that many companies have found helpful is developing a simple in-house, videotape-based certification program for all users. This does not have to be a high-cost program.

Forecasting Service Parts Demand

Forecasting Models

A good forecasting system is essential to a good inventory planning and control system. Most forecasting systems for inventory planning implement an approach to forecasting called "exponential smoothing." Several types of exponential smoothing models are available, including:

1. Simple exponential smoothing (no trend and no seasonality).
2. Exponential smoothing with trend.
3. Exponential smoothing with seasonality.
4. Exponential smoothing with trend and seasonality. (This is also called the "Winter model" after a researcher named Peter Winter who developed the original idea. This is the most popular approach.)

A company could selectively implement any one of the above four forecasting models for each and every item in the inventory, or could implement the "Winter model" (exponential smoothing with both trend and seasonal factors) for all items. Those items that have no trend in the data will have a zero trend component. Similarly, those items that have no seasonality in the data will have all multiplicative seasonality factors of 1.0.

The Winter model is probably the best approach for most companies. The disadvantage of using the Winter model for all items is that it requires more data storage and more input/output, but, with modern computer technology, these are not important issues. More details on forecasting with exponential smoothing models can be found in an appendix to this chapter.

The Lumpy Demand Problem

A serious problem with all exponential smoothing models (and with most other forecasting models as well) is the problem of "lumpy demand." An item with lumpy demand typically has many zero demand periods. For example, the following monthly service part demand is clearly "lumpy":

J	F	M	A	M	J	J	A	S	O	N	D
80	0	0	0	0	90	0	0	0	10	1	0

Lumpy demand is a particularly common problem with service parts because so many parts are slow moving and have a demand pattern with many zeros and a few ones and twos.

Simple exponential smoothing handles lumpy demand very poorly. For example, if the exponential smoothing model makes a forecast of 80 for January (a perfect forecast), the forecast for February will also be 80. The forecasts for March, April, and May will also be much higher than 0. In May, the forecast for June will be almost down to 0; unfortunately, the demand in June is high again. As this example demonstrates, exponential smoothing for lumpy demand can be very bad. It forecasts high when the demand is low and forecasts low when the demand is high. A researcher named Crowston developed an improved version of the exponential smoothing that forecasts both the time between orders and the size of the order. Although this model has been in the literature for many years, few organizations have implemented the concept.

DEC handles lumpy demand simply by using a moving average and a trend. The trend is based on the machine population. This simple approach seems to work well for their purposes. Given the problems with exponential smoothing for items with lumpy demand, this may be the only viable approach for many to use.

Many organizations forecast using monthly time periods. Others forecast in weekly or daily periods. Obviously, smaller time buckets allow for more detailed data. However, smaller time buckets also mean more data storage, more computer time, and potentially more crowded screens. Smaller time buckets will also create more lumpiness in the data. Many service organizations find that a weekly time bucket is satisfactory for most purposes. It is possible to forecast on a weekly basis and still measure replenishment lead times in days.

Forecasting Lifetime Demand

It is possible to forecast the expected lifetime demand. This is the cumulative demand from the current date through the product termination date. It is also possible to forecast the demand to the "end of time" if the demand is decreasing and no termination date is known. (Note that if the forecast has a zero slope or has an upward slope, the forecast to the end of time will be infinity.) The forecast of the lifetime demand is very useful for "final buy" decisions and for determining how much inventory is not really needed. Both of these issues are discussed later in this chapter.

Brown (1982) and others (Hill, Giard, and Mabert, 1991) have found that once demand begins a steady decline, it generally follows an exponential decay model. In other words, the demand in period t is a percentage β times the demand in period $t-1$. The percentage β tends to be fairly constant over time. The exponential decay model is then:

$$d_t = \beta d_{t-1}$$

where d_t is the demand in period t and β is the percentage remaining from period to period.

If a part has a definite termination date, the forecast of lifetime demand (cumulative demand) is simply the sum of the forecasts through the termination date. However, if the part does not have a definite termination date, the following model can be used to forecast the lifetime demand for a service part through the end of time (the cumulative demand from now to infinity):

$$D = d\beta/(1-\beta)$$

where D is the estimate of the expected lifetime demand, d is the recent average demand (possibly a moving average or the current exponentially smoothed average), and β is the slope of the demand when plotted on semi-log paper. This is sometimes called the "all-time" demand (or "all-time" supply). A short derivation for the above equation can be found in an appendix.

When forecasting for the next period ahead or forecasting for the lifetime demand, the forecast should be accompanied by an estimate of the standard deviation of the forecast error so that intelligent estimates can be made of the highest reasonable lifetime demand. The author has researched this subject and developed a practical approach for estimating both the forecast and the forecast interval for lifetime demand. The article by Hill, Mabert, and Giard presents these ideas.

Exponential smoothing-based forecasts perform very well for most service parts inventory systems (at least for the fast-moving parts). These forecasts can be used to directly feed reorder point, safety stock, and order quantity calculations. However, it is very important that the users have some means of controlling the systems. Specifically, exception reports are needed to signal problems such as:

The demand (sales) in one particular period is much higher or lower than forecasted.

The demand (sales) is consistently higher or lower than forecasted.

The first problem is found by means of a "demand filter" and the second problem is found by a "tracking signal." Each of these will be briefly discussed below.

Demand Filter

When the actual demand (sales) for a period is entered, a check is made to verify that the actual value is within a reasonable tolerance of the forecast. The tolerance limits are set by taking the forecast plus or minus Z standard deviations of the forecast error where Z is the standard normal deviate (usually close to 3). If the actual demand (sales) is unusually high or low, it is important to find out why this happened because this might be useful information. The problem could be bad data or an exceptionally large order. In either case, it is important to learn from the situation and take appropriate action. The equations for the demand filter are in an appendix to this chapter.

Tracking Signal

Forecasts are very often incorrect, but the positive and negative errors generally balance each other out so that the average error (also called the "bias") is near zero. However, when sales are going up or down very quickly, exponential smoothing models often lag behind and develop a significant bias. When this happens, it is important that the user be given an exception report that identifies all items with a large bias. The user should study the demand (sales) pattern for each item that has a large bias in the forecast error and then:

1. Try to learn why the demand is changing so rapidly (discontinued item, etc.). This unusual condition provides an opportunity to learn something. The user may want to double check the input data to make sure it is not a data entry problem.
2. Manually adjust the current exponentially smoothed average or adjust the smoothing constant. Sometimes temporarily

increasing the smoothing constant will allow the forecasting model to adjust to the new demand conditions.

3. Consider canceling orders, changing order quantities, rescheduling orders, or scrapping some inventory if necessary.

The equations for the tracking signal are developed in an appendix to this chapter. The implementation of the equations is very simple. Whenever the tracking signal for an item is greater than some critical value, an exception report is displayed for the analyst. The items in this report should be sorted by tracking signal values so that the biggest problems are addressed first. The critical value should be set based on historical experience. Typical values are in the range of 3 to 6. (Unfortunately, there is no easy way to set these limits because the tracking signal does not follow a known distribution.) It is a good idea to adjust the critical value in order to keep the number of items in the report to a manageable size.

Reorder Points and Safety Stocks

The reorder point is used to trigger a replenishment order from the factory or vendor for a part. Some companies set the reorder point intuitively based on experience. Other companies use a simple approach such as setting the reorder point as the inventory required to cover the average demand over the next X weeks where X is generally in the range of the lead time plus two to four weeks. These informal approaches do not explicitly take into account the variability of the demand. An appendix to this chapter describes both a simple and a sophisticated approach for determining reorder points based on the variability of the demand during lead time.

The concept of a "critical level" is not found in any of the major inventory management or inventory theory textbooks. However, the concept is widely used in practice for service parts inventories. The basic concept is that users want a warning whenever an item is just about to run out. The warning should be early enough so that users can call the vendor to expedite the order if necessary.

This critical level concept has several problems. First, when the critical level is hit, a phone call is often made to the vendor only to find out that the order will be shipped and received on time as per the original agreement. This obviously does not add value to the company.

Second, it is possible that the user will receive exception notices related to the critical level on a very large percentage of the orders. This is particularly true for items with a critical level at or below the safety stock level. (Recall that, with a reorder point system, the average inventory on hand when an order is received is the safety stock quantity.)

Third, it is not clear how to determine the critical level. Should the critical level be set at two weeks of average demand? Set at the safety stock level? Set at the worst case demand over two weeks? Probably the best and simplest way to handle this is to set the critical level as dT where d is the exponentially smoothed average demand per period and T is the number of days needed to express mail the item.

Purchase Order Quantities

The well-known and often maligned economic order quantity (EOQ) is the order quantity that minimizes the sum of the total expected carrying cost and order cost. In other words, this is the order quantity that best balances the cost of carrying inventory and the cost of placing an order. If the order quantity is too large, the carrying cost will be very large. If the order quantity is too small, too many orders will be required and the cost of placing many orders will be too large. The expected total annual cost (ignoring all fixed costs) is:

$$TC = (D/Q)S + (Q/2)hc + Dc$$

where,

TC = Expected total annual cost related to ordering and carrying inventory.

D = Annual demand (sales) in units.

Q = Order quantity in units.

S = Marginal cost to place an order. (This includes the marginal cost to receive the order.)

h = Carrying charge (decimal percent). (This is the cost of carrying $1 of inventory for one year.)

c = Unit cost.

D/Q is the expected number of orders placed per year and $(D/Q)S$ is the average annual order cost. $Q/2$ is the average inventory in units, $(Q/2)c$ is the average inventory investment in dollars, and $(Q/2)hc$ is the average carrying cost per year. This assumes that the demand is fairly constant. Dc is the total procurement cost for the item for the year. Applying calculus, the optimal economic order quantity (the EOQ can be found to be:

$$EOQ = \sqrt{\frac{2SD}{hc}} \tag{1}$$

It is important to remember that the total cost function above is not very sensitive to errors in the order quantity. In other words, an order quantity that is not very different from the economic order quantity will not affect the total cost significantly. It is also important to understand that h (the carrying charge parameter) is very difficult to determine with any degree of precision. It should be at least as great as the cost of capital. When storage space is at a premium, it should be much larger than the cost of capital. As a result, many organizations view h as a policy parameter that should be adjusted by management to either increase or decrease cycle inventory investment.

When determining S (the order cost parameter), it is important to remember that this should be an incremental cost. Overhead costs, such as the cost of the warehouse manager, do not vary with the number of purchase orders and should not be considered when determining the value of S. A simple form for estimating the order cost can be found in an appendix to this chapter.

The above total cost equation can be used to evaluate quantity discounts. The procedure (in its simplest form) requires the evaluation of the total cost (TC) for the EOQ for each price alternative and at each break point. The best of these alternatives is then selected. Note that some alternatives may be infeasible and should be ignored. For example, if $c =$ \$20 for an order quantity greater than 100 units and the EOQ is 80 when $c =$ \$20, then $Q = 80$ is not a feasible alternative.

Probably the most important issue to remember about the economic order quantity is that, in the real world, it is very difficult to estimate the parameters and that the assumptions of constant price and constant demand are often not valid. As a result, the economic order quantity should be looked at as a starting point for determining order quantities rather than the magical "right" answer.

First and Last Lot Buys

The first lot buy (initial provisioning) is usually based on a forecast of the sales over the first few months that a new product will be in the field. The manufacturer and/or service engineer should be able to help make these decisions.

When making a decision on the last lot buy (final lot buy) for a part, it is necessary to make trade-offs between two costs:

The cost of having too much inventory, and, therefore, having to carry and scrap some parts.

The cost of having too little inventory, and, therefore, having to repurchase (or rebuild) additional parts.

In the simplest form, this problem is called the "newsboy" problem. It is formulated and solved mathematically in an appendix to this chapter.

SERVICE PARTS WAREHOUSE INVENTORY MANAGEMENT

Managing a service parts inventory involves many activities. The inventory management activities described in this book include:

- Scrapping obsolete inventory.
- Part numbering.
- Cycle counting.
- Warranty returns.
- Parts kits.
- Bar coding.

Scrapping Obsolete Inventory

Ideally, no service parts inventory will ever have any obsolete inventory at the end of a product life cycle. Of course in the real world, service parts inventories often have many items that are obsolete.

Identifying obsolete inventory is a nontrivial job. The basic approaches include:

The R&D Method.   The R&D method simply means to physically walk around and look for "rust and dust," which indicate parts have been on the shelf for a long time. This unscientific method has limited applicability but can be a useful consulting/auditing technique and even occasionally makes for a good joke.

Days Since Last Use.   Showing a ranked list of items to knowledgeable managers and/or analysts is all that many organizations need in order to make decisions regarding which items to carry.

Number of Days of Supply.   The number of days (or weeks) of supply is calculated simply by taking the current on-hand inventory and dividing by the current average (or exponentially smoothed average) usage rate. Again, simply presenting a ranked list of items to managers or analysts can often provide sufficient information for determining which items to carry.

Forecasting Lifetime Demand.   Forecasting both the mean and variance of the lifetime demand can provide very useful information used to determine how much inventory to scrap at any time during the life of the parts. Scrapping the inventory now rather than later has "time value of money" advantages. The concept here is that the inventory that is scrapped is inventory that is clearly in excess of the worst-case lifetime demand. (The issue of forecasting lifetime demand was discussed earlier in this chapter.)

Obsolete inventory can be disposed in many different ways including:

Throw it into the trash.

Destroy it with chemicals or explosives.

Sell it for salvage value.

Sell it back to the vendor or manufacturer.

Recycle it.

Management should consider both legal and ethical issues when disposing of hazardous materials. This is an issue of growing concern for many organizations as well as for government. Some manufacturers have been very creative in finding profitable ways to dispose of waste materials that also protect the environment.

The author of this book developed an effective decision support system (DSS) for this problem for 3M Service Parts and Logistics Center. This DSS is described in the 3M case study at the end of this chapter and in an article by Hill, Mabert, and Giard referenced at the end of this book. The DSS makes use of the inventory analysts' experience while still employing a sophisticated set of models for forecasting and inventory planning.

Part Numbering

Part numbering is a controversial issue. Nearly everyone agrees that all controlled parts should have one, and only one, part number and that each number should only be used once. However, many people disagree on the length of part numbers and how much meaning should be packed into the part numbering system.

Most companies use very long part numbers in order to try to get as much meaning as possible into the number. However, data entry without the help of bar codes is very error prone. Most experts agree that it is better to have shorter (say five- or six-digit) part numbers to increase data accuracy. Users can enter the short part number and have the computer system display vast amounts of additional information about the part. Sophisticated coding schemes are now available to classify parts very accurately. A shorter part number makes it much easier for people with a short memory buffer to store the number in memory and then accurately enter it into the computer.

Most companies also mix both alpha and numeric characters in their part numbers. This presents many problems for communicating both verbally and visually. For example, for verbal communication, the following pairs of letters sound alike: A and K, M and N, and E and V. For written communication, many letters and numbers are easy to confuse (e.g., 1 and L, 0 and O, 5 and S, U and V, 2 and Z). Although a minority of organizations seem to be doing this, most experts agree that it is better to use only numeric characters in part numbers. This also helps with voice recognition devices for data entry.

A check digit may be added to the end of all numeric part numbers in order to screen out common data entry errors. The check digit is computed from the first segment of the part number and becomes the last digit of the part number. Simple algorithms are available for determining the check digit for a part number and for screening part numbers upon data entry to be sure that they satisfy the check digit requirements. A check digit can help eliminate the majority of data entry errors.

It should be noted at this point that, despite the fact that these part numbering concepts have been in the literature and discussed at APICS conferences for many years, few companies have implemented them. Evidently, inertia on this subject is hard to overcome. The companies that have implemented these concepts have found that it is best to apply the new part numbering rules only to new parts, rather than trying to renumber thousands of parts already in the system.

Cycle Counting

The traditional approach to maintaining service parts inventory records accuracy has been to conduct a year-end physical inventory. This was often required for financial reporting, with the goal of ensuring that the total inventory balance was correct. The year-end physical inventory was often riddled with errors made by inexperienced people who were not highly motivated to maintain data accuracy. This process often required a warehouse shutdown and had little or no accountability for the people involved in the process.

A better approach to ensuring record accuracy is to ''cycle count'' a subset of the inventory throughout the year. This approach uses experienced people and imposes accountability on the process. Whereas the goal of the year-end physical inventory is to correct inventory balances, the goal of cycle counting is to identify and solve process problems that cause inaccurate balances. All first-class inventory systems use cycle counting.

Implementation of a cycle counting system could take many forms. The process often begins by determining the number of items to be counted per day (number of cycle counters × number of parts counted per day). From there, any of the following rules could be used to determine when to count the on-hand inventory balance:

- ABC counting frequency. Count the A items once per month, the B items once per quarter, and the C items once per year.

- Count just before the release of an order. This can possibly avoid an unneeded order. The on-hand balance should be fairly low at this point (something less than the reorder point).

- Count just before a receipt is added to the inventory. This is a good time because the on-hand inventory should be very low and the stock picker is already at the location. This system also counts the fast-moving items more often. The fast-moving items are more prone to error simply because they have more transactions.

- Count when the on-hand hits zero (or negative). It should be very easy to count "air." Negative inventory balances are common and should be checked in order to immediately fix the obvious problem.

- Count by location. This makes sense from a walking/travel time point of view.

- Count with pick ticket. The pick ticket can be used to instruct the stock pickers to take an inventory count at the time that an order is filled.

- Control group of parts. Some companies have defined a control group of parts that is thought to be representative of the larger inventory. These parts are counted on a regular basis in order to assess overall inventory performance in much the same way as the Dow-Jones Average uses a control group of companies to measure overall stock market performance.

When counting on-hand inventories, an item count is considered accurate if the balance on-hand is within counting tolerance. The counting tolerance for a large barrel of washers might be fairly large, whereas, the counting tolerance for engines might be zero.

The concept of cycle counting can be applied to field service data other than just warehouse inventories. For example, cycle counting can be applied to vehicle stock as well as a warehouse inventory.

Warranty Returns

Many field service organizations provide parts that are warranted by parts manufacturers. Effective management of warranty returns for these parts can have a significant impact on overall field service profitability. The challenge here is to keep track of the warranty date for all items by serial number as well as by part number so that the warranty can be reclaimed.

Parts Kits

A "parts kit" is a set of parts that is often used together on a emergency maintenance or preventive maintenance service call. The advantage of having kits is that it makes it easier for the technician to grab a kit and head out for the repair. However, the disadvantage is that not all of the parts are required for all repairs and the technician is left with several extra parts and no place to put them and no system to track them. Ideally, parts kits are designed so that the probability of having a "broken call" (a call that is not completed due to missing parts) is minimized subject to a budget constraint on the investment in the parts kit.

Bar Coding

The 3M Service Parts and Logistics Center case is a good example of a service parts bar coding system. This case illustrates how bar coding can be used to achieve very efficient stocking, stock picking, packing, and shipping operations due to fast and accurate data collection.

Bar coding can be of value for activities outside the warehouse. For example, customer machines can have a bar code to help the technician quickly access the machine history in the computer. Bar coding can also have great value in the field for controlling service parts.

SERVICE PARTS LOGISTICS INVENTORY MANAGEMENT

A significant portion of a service parts inventory is often carried in the field in regional warehouses, branch offices, and technician vehicles. These inventories often consist of only small amounts of frequently used parts.

The following discussion is presented in the context of determining the correct amount of inventory to have in a technician vehicle. However, these concepts can easily be expanded to analyze other types of inventories as well.

Inventory carried in the technician's vehicle is sometimes called "car stock" or "custody inventory." The factors that must be considered in determining the best stocking levels for a technician's vehicle inventory include:

- Technician training. Technicians should only carry parts for models for which they are trained and certified to repair.
- Failure rate for the model in the technician's territory. This may be based on the known machine population in the territory.
- Failure rate for the part. Obviously, some parts fail more often than others.
- Cost of the part. The higher the cost, the less likely that it will be economical for the technician to carry the part.
- Size of the part. Vehicle space is a scarce commodity that has an opportunity cost associated with it.

The car stock target inventory for a technician can be viewed as a newsboy problem (discussed above) where the overage cost (c_o) is the cost of carrying inventory over the year, and the underage cost (c_u) is the cost of the lost goodwill, labor cost for a return call, expediting cost for acquiring the part, and so forth.

Another aspect of field service logistics inventory management is the idea of cooperative agreements for service parts between two or more companies in one region. For example, some power generation utilities in the United States work together with other utilities to pool high-cost critical service parts in order to reduce carrying cost and decrease stockout risk. A similar idea is pursued for backup of some major computer systems. This concept seems to have potential for many other self-maintainer organizations.

REPAIRABLE INVENTORY MANAGEMENT

Repairable inventories can have a very significant impact on the total materials cost for a field service organization. For example, Digital Equipment Corporation (DEC) saves about 50 percent of its annual materials cost by repairing boards that are returned from the field. Repairable inventories can be repaired by:

> The customer at the customer's location.
>
> The field service technician at the customer's location or at the technician's home location.
>
> A technician at a repair depot.
>
> A technician at the factory.
>
> A "fourth-party" repair service.

Many companies have a repair depot or repair shop, where failed units are sent for repair. The trend in the United States is for these to be centralized in one place. For example, a large third-party maintainer does all major repairs on computer monitors in one central location.

Repairable inventories are often managed with a "rebuild-exchange program." When a unit fails in the field, the service organization immediately sends out a good unit to replace the failed one. The failed unit is returned to the repair shop. Incoming failed units can either be repaired directly or broken down into modules or components which may be refurbished separately. Complete units are then reassembled from refurbished and new components. In some cases, it is necessary for the repaired component to be returned to the original unit. This is done by matching the serial number for the component with the serial number for the unit.

A rebuild-exchange program has advantages for both the customer and the service provider. The customer does not have to wait for the repair and, therefore, is buffered from the variability of demand. This allows for higher utilization and better productivity for the repair shop.

A repair shop is different from a job shop in that a great deal of testing must take place. Policies must be defined regarding what to test, what to refurbish, and how to refurbish or repair each component. For example, the policy may be to always replace a particular component without bothering to test it.

One of the most important and difficult problems in this environment is finding the right balance between service levels and inventory investment for units and/or components. This is a difficult problem, given the variability of the demand and the variability of repair times. Many academic research articles have been devoted to this problem. For an example, see Chua, Scudder, and Hill (1992) for more information on the problem. The problem is particularly important for aircraft engines and other expensive repairable units where both the carrying and the stockout costs are extremely high.

A repair shop does have some similarities to a job shop, and some just-in-time (JIT) principles may be useful here. JIT concepts for a repair shop include:

1. Minimize setup times (and costs) so that lot sizes can be kept low. This tends to minimize the mean flow time for parts, which in turn tends to minimize the mean downtime for failed units.
2. Keep lot sizes small. The ideal lot size is one unit. Small lot sizes also tend to minimize flow times, make quality problems easier to find, and minimize downtime for failed units.
3. Eliminate wasted movement. Most repair shops waste a large percentage of time with materials handling, looking for tools, etc. As Suzaki (1987) notes, workplace organization is important to setup time efficiency.

4. Increase ownership of the quality of each operation. This can be done by job enlargement wherein a person or a work group takes responsibility for a set of parts.

5. Eliminate all nonvalue added activities such as unnecessary paperwork, unnecessary inspection, etc.

Just-in-time principles are discussed in much more detail in the text by Vollmann, Berry, and Whybark and in the book by Suzaki.

PRICING SERVICE PARTS

Service parts typically have high margins. Margins are often in the range of 20 percent to 500 percent of the cost. Although some companies have a standard markup across all parts, many increase the margin as the product progresses through its life cycle. As a product reaches the end of its life, the margins are increased to reflect the higher cost of keeping the parts for an older model and to give the customer added incentive to change over to a newer model.

Prices for service parts are also affected by market conditions. If the company has a proprietary product and proprietary service parts for this product, the market may be willing to bear a higher price for the product.

Ideally, the service parts should reflect the order processing cost for the part. For example, a small $.50 part might have an order processing cost of $30 to pick, pack, ship, and invoice. Some companies will charge $.50 for this order; others will charge $30.50, and others will charge something in between. Another approach to this issue is to have a minimum order size.

CONCLUSIONS

Service parts management is often far more complex than managing a typical distribution inventory. Service parts management involves managing a complex network of warehouse and distribution inventories, warranty returns, repairable inventories, slow-moving items, obsolescence problems.

Service parts management systems must interface to many other organizations including manufacturing (for service parts planning), accounting (for pricing, billing, accounts receivable, and accounts payable), information systems (for application systems development), and engineering (for engineering change order information). In some companies, purchasing is handled by a central purchasing group, which acts as a representative for the service parts group. Many companies have a new awareness of problems with disposal of hazardous products and therefore must interface to a centralized hazardous waste group.

Service parts inventories are a major investment for most field service organizations. Careful attention to managing these inventories can yield substantial benefits in terms of both better service and lower costs—which can result in improved customer satisfaction and organizational profitability.

APPENDIX 6.1   FORECASTING WITH EXPONENTIAL SMOOTHING

Definitions

α	=	Smoothing constant $(0 < \alpha < 1)$. Pronounced "alpha."
$A(t)$	=	Exponentially smoothed average at the end of period T.
β	=	Smoothing constant for trend $(0 < \beta < 1)$. Pronounced "beta."
$D(t)$	=	Actual demand (sales) in period t (in units).
$F(t + n)$	=	Forecast for n periods ahead. (For example, $F(t + 1)$ is the forecast made at the end of period t for period $t + 1$.)
m	=	Number of periods in a year. (When using monthly periods, m should be 12.)
n	=	Number of periods ahead that are to be forecasted.
$R(t - m)$	=	Multiplicative seasonal index found $(t - m)$ periods ago (e.g., last year).

γ $\quad$ = Smoothing constant for seasonality ($0 < \gamma < 1$). Pronounced "gamma."

$T(t-1)$ $\quad$ = Trend as of the end of period $t-1$.

Equations

The equations for the Winter model (exponential smoothing with trend and seasonal factors) are written below. At the end of period t, the value for the actual demand for this period, $D(t)$, becomes available. The following equations are then used to make a forecast for period $t + n$:

$$A(t) \quad = \alpha \, D(t)/R(t-m) + (1-\alpha)\,[A(t-1) + T(t-1)]$$
$$T(t) \quad = \beta\,[A(t) - A(t-1)] + (1-\beta)\,T(t-1)$$
$$R(t) \quad = \gamma\,D(t)/A(t) + (1-\gamma)\,R(t-m)$$
$$F(t+n) = [A(t) + nT(t)]\,R(t+n-m)$$

The first equation updates the underlying average. The second equation updates the trend. The third equation updates the seasonal factor that will be used next year. The fourth equation makes the forecast for the demand n periods ahead (n is usually set to 1).

Finding the Best Parameters for the Model

Direct search methods can be applied to quickly find the optimal (least squares) parameters for virtually any forecasting model. This method can be used to update the parameters on a regular basis, if desired. If the resources are not available to run the experiments needed to find the best parameters, the following guidelines might be of some help in finding reasonable estimates of these parameters:

1. Alpha (α) should be between 0.1 and 0.3. When the time series is stationary, exponential smoothing and an n period moving average are equivalent when $\alpha = 2/(n+1)$.
2. Beta (β) should be between 0.1 and 0.4.
3. Gamma (γ) should be between 0.1 and 0.3.

Initialization

Several initialization issues need to be addressed with any forecasting model. All of the variables that are exponentially smoothed have to be initialized. The recommended initial values for the exponentially smoothed values are:

$A(t)$ = Recent average sales (demand) or simply the last actual sales value in the database. This value will not have much impact over the longer run.

$T(t)$ = Recent trend or simply 0.

$R(t)$ = Ratio of the seasonal values to the annual average over the last year. A "centered moving average" is a good way to do this.

APPENDIX 6.2   ALL-TIME DEMAND FOR EXPONENTIALLY DECAYING DEMAND

We seek to derive a simple expression for the cumulative demand for a service part through "all time" (from now to infinity) given that the demand is decaying exponentially. We define d_t as the actual demand in period t. β is the decimal percent of the demand that remains from one period to the next.

We assume that $d_t = \beta d_{t-1}$. The cumulative demand through all-time is then:

$$\sum_{t=1}^{\infty} d_t = \sum_{t=1}^{\infty} \beta d_{t-1} = \beta d_0 + \beta^2 d_0 + \beta^3 d_0 + \ldots + \beta^k d_0 + \ldots + \beta^{\infty} d_0$$

$$= d_0 \sum_{t=1}^{\infty} \beta_t$$

$$= d_0 \beta / (1 - \beta)$$

The last step is based on a common infinite series formula. This step is only valid when $\beta < 1$. The parameter d_0 is the current (time 0) demand.

APPENDIX 6.3   TRACKING SIGNALS AND DEMAND FILTERS

Definitions

$E(t)$ = Forecast error in period t.

$SE(t)$ = Smoothed average error at the end of period t. This is an estimate of the recent average error and is, therefore, an estimate of the bias. It should be initialized at zero.

$SAE(t)$ = Smoothed average absolute error at the end of period t. This is an estimate of the average size of the forecast error without regard to the sign. Note that $|x|$ is the absolute value of x. Should be initialized at 1.

$SMSE(t)$ = Smoothed mean squared error. This is an estimate of the variance of the error. The square root of the $SMSE(t)$, therefore, is an estimate of the standard deviation of the forecast error. This estimate of the standard deviation of the forecast error should be used in the safety stock calculation. It should be initialized at zero.

$RSE(t)$ = Running sum of the error. This is simply the cumulative error over time. Ideally this will be zero as the positive and negative errors should balance each other out if the model is unbiased. It should be initialized at zero.

$TS(t)$ = The tracking signal value at the end of period t. If the absolute value of the tracking signal is large (say over 4), a tracking signal exception report should be created.

$DF(t)$ = The demand filter value at the end of period t. If the absolute value of the demand filter is large (say over 3), a demand filter exception report should be created.

Equations

The following equations are useful for the tracking signal, demand filter, and safety stock calculations:

$$E(t) = D(t) - F(t)$$
$$SE(t) = \alpha E(t) + (1-\alpha)SE(t)$$
$$SAE(t) = \alpha|E(t)| + (1-\alpha)SAE(t)$$
$$SMSE(t) = \alpha E(t)^2 + (1-\alpha)SMSE(t)$$
$$RSE(t) = RSE(t) + E(t)$$
$$TS(t) = |RSE(t)|/SAE(t)$$
$$DF(t) = E(t)/SMSE(t)^{1/2}$$

Note: $SMSE(t)^{1/2}$ is the square root of $SMSE(t)$.

Demand Filter

The demand filter exception report is presented whenever $DF(t)$ for an item exceeds some critical value. With some reasonable assumptions,

DF(t) can be treated as a standard normal random variable (a normally distributed random variable with mean of zero and a standard deviation of one). The period to period fluctuations in demand will rarely result in a *DF(t)* value less than −3 or greater than 3. If *DF(t)* exceeds these limits, it is an indication that the demand value in period *t* deserves some attention.

Tracking Signal
The tracking signal is "tripped" whenever the value *TS(t)* is greater than some critical value *TS**. *TS** is typically set to some value in the range of 3 to 6 depending on how closely management wants to monitor forecast error bias and how many items the inventory analyst can handle.

APPENDIX 6.4   REORDER POINT CALCULATIONS

The reorder point is an important parameter for most independent demand inventory systems. Whereas the order quantity is relatively easy to determine intuitively, the reorder point is not nearly as easy to determine because it requires an estimate of the standard deviation of demand and it requires a difficult carrying cost/stockout cost tradeoff.

The reorder point should be set at the average demand over lead time plus the safety stock. The equation for this is:

$$R = dL + SS$$

where,

R = Reorder point (in units). When the inventory position gets to this level, a new order is triggered.

d = Average demand per period. The exponentially smoothed average demand could be used here.

L = Planned replenishment lead time. This should be greater than the average lead time.

SS = Safety stock (in units).

Safety stock calculations are particularly important for service parts because so much of the inventory is tied up in safety stock. Safety stock can be computed as:

$$SS = k\sigma_L$$

where,

k = The safety factor. The safety factor controls the safety stock level in order to achieve a desired service level. k is usually between 1 and 3.

σ = The standard deviation of the demand per period. Technically, this is the estimate of the standard deviation of the demand per period. This can be determined from the square root of the smoothed mean squared error from the exponential smoothing model. The standard deviation of the demand per period can be estimated with the sample standard deviation:

$$\sigma = \left[\sum_{t=1}^{N} (d_t - d)^2/(N-1) \right] = \left[[(\sum_{t=1}^{N} d^2) - Nd^2]/(N-1) \right]^{1/2}$$

where d is the average demand, d_t is the actual demand in period t, and N is the number of periods of available data. The first expression is the definitional form. The second expression above is called the "computational form" and can be computed in one pass on the data.

σ_L = Standard deviation of the demand over the lead time. This is often estimated with $L^p\sigma$ where σ is the standard deviation of the demand per period and p is in the range of .5 to .7. When p = .5, L^p is simply the square root of L. The value of p = .7 is better as it accounts for the fact that the demand from period to period is not serially independent.

The simplest procedure for determining the safety factor k is based on the probability of stocking out during any one order cycle. An order cycle is the time between the receipt of an order and the time of the next order. If a part has a demand of D units per year, and Q units are ordered each time, the number of order cycles per year is D/Q. Typical values for k using this procedure are displayed below.

k	Service Level
0.00	50.0%
1.00	84.1%
1.50	93.3%
1.65	95.0%
2.00	97.7%
2.50	99.4%
2.80	99.7%
3.00	99.9%

For example, there will be a 95.5 percent probability of not stocking out on one order cycle if the safety factor is set to $k = 1.65$. Although this procedure is found in most introductory operations management textbooks, it does not define the service level the same way that most service parts inventory managers define it. The above procedure implicitly defines the service level as the probability that a stockout will not occur on any one order cycle. This does not take into account how many order cycles will occur during a year and does not take into account how many units might be stocked out on any one order cycle.

A much more meaningful service level measure is the "expected fill rate." This is the expected number of units filled from stock over the order cycle divided by the expected number of units demanded during the order cycle. This procedure is as follows:

Step 1: Specify the order quantity Q, the desired service level (fill rate) SL, and the standard deviation of the demand during lead time σ_L. (Note that this is not the standard deviation of the demand per period.)

Step 2: Use the following equation to find G:

$$G = Q(1 - SL)/\sigma_L$$

where,

G = Partial expectation. This is the expected number of units stocked out on each order cycle based on the standard normal distribution. (This assumes that the demand itself follows a normal distribution. $\sigma_L G$ is the expected number of units stocked out on each order cycle.)

Q = The order quantity for the item.

SL = Desired service level specified by the user as described above.

σ_L = Standard deviation of the demand over the lead time (estimated from historical data).

Step 3: Now that G is known, H and k can be estimated from the following approximation:

$$H = -1.75294$$
$$+ 0.4442135G$$
$$- 0.07061455G^2$$
$$- 0.17592241/(G + 0.044212641)$$
$$- 0.0012267386/(G + 0.00030570313)$$
$$k = (G - 0.39894228)\,H$$

This value of k will provide (on average) a service level of "SL." k is usually restricted to non-negative values.

Step 4: Now that k is known, calculate the safety stock and reorder point as before with $R = dL + SS$ and $SS = k\sigma_L$.

This procedure for determining safety stocks and reorder points provides a service level that is much more meaningful than the simplistic procedure presented above. Although this procedure may seem complex, it is very simple to implement on a computer.

An example to help illustrate these concepts might be useful at this point. Given the following information on a single independent demand item, the problem is to find the *EOQ* and the reorder point.

Weekly demand in past 10 weeks:	9,1,6,5,8,0,2,4,1,3
Desired service level:	99%
Carrying charge:	30% (or .30)
Order cost:	$50 per order
Unit cost:	$400 per unit
Number of weeks/year:	52 weeks
Lead time:	2 weeks

From the above demand time series, the following values can be computed:

Average demand per week:	3.9 units/week
Standard deviation of demand/week:	3.071373 units/week
Standard deviation of demand/L:	$L^{.7}\sigma = 4.98946$
Economic order quantity:	13 units
Simple procedure:	
Safety factor:	2.0
Safety stock:	10 units
Reorder point:	18 units
Fill rate procedure:	
Safety factor:	1.1649
Safety stock:	6 units
Reorder point:	14 units

Notice that in this example, the expected fill rate procedure has a safety stock that is 40 percent lower than the simple procedure. Depending on the input parameters, safety stocks for the expected fill rate procedure may be lower or higher than for the simple procedure. The only generalizable statement that can be made here is that the expected fill rate procedure will provide safety stocks that will achieve service levels much closer to the desired fill rate.

Time Phased Order Point

The time phased order point (TPOP) is an extension of the reorder point logic to situations where the demand during lead time is not constant. TPOP makes the most sense in situations when the demand has a trend or seasonal pattern or the demand is lumpy (but known in advance) due to customer orders.

When forecasting nonconstant demand, the expected demand during lead time is not dL. Given the safety stock inventory level (SS), TPOP simulates the demand to determine when the inventory position will hit the safety stock level. The planned start date for the order is found by back scheduling from this time. The safety stock for the time phased reorder point is the same as the simple reorder point safety stock.

The time phased reorder point procedure is as follows:

Step 1:   Define I as the current inventory position (units on hand plus on order) and set t to the period number for the next period.

Step 2:   Forecast for period t and set $I = I - F_t$, where F_t is the forecasted demand (sales) for period t. If the new I is greater than the predetermined safety stock quantity, set $t = t + 1$ and repeat Step 2; otherwise, move on to Step 3.

Step 3:   The projected inventory position is expected to cut into the safety stock in period t. It is necessary, therefore, to plan an order release in period $T = t - L$ where L is the planned lead time. If T is at or before the current date, then release an order. If T is before the current date, then create an exception report.

APPENDIX 6.5   POISSON DISTRIBUTION FOR ITEMS WITH LOW DEMAND

When an item has low demand, the demand per period often follows the poisson distribution. Equation (2) uses the poisson distribution to compute the probability $p(x)$ of having a demand of exactly x units given that the mean (average) demand rate is λ units per period. Note that x can only take on integer values.

$$p(x) = \frac{e^{-\lambda}\lambda^x}{x!} \tag{2}$$

Equation (3) computes $F(x)$ which is the probability of having a demand of x or fewer units given that the mean demand rate is λ units/period. $p(x)$ is said to be the probability mass function whereas $F(x)$ is said to be the distribution function.

$$F(x) = e^{-\lambda} \sum_{i=0}^{i=x} \frac{\lambda^i}{i!} \tag{3}$$

When the λ is greater than 9, it is generally considered safe to approximate the poisson distribution with a normal distribution. Unfortunately, the normal distribution does not have a simple equation that we can use to compute probabilities as does the poisson distribution. For the normal distribution it is necessary to resort to tables or approximate equations.

APPENDIX 6.6   WORK SHEET FOR ESTIMATING THE ORDER COST PARAMETER

Background

When computing the optimal order quantity for an item based on the economic trade-off between order cost and carrying cost, it is necessary to have an estimate of the cost to place an order for that item. This document gives some practical advice on how to approach this nontrivial task.

When a buyer decides to make a purchase, many things have to happen. These include:

Create the purchase order.

Communicate the purchase order to the vendor.

Ship the order.

Receive the order and move to storage.

Process the vendor invoice for the purchase order.

Marginal (Incremental) Costs

When estimating the cost to order an item for the purpose of determining an optimal order quantity, it is very important to remember to include only the costs that vary with the number of purchase orders over the short run. Only marginal costs should be included; all fixed and overhead costs should be excluded.

For example, the company's electric bill will be the same if the number of purchase orders is increased by 10 percent. Electric bills and all other overhead costs are, therefore, irrelevant to the order cost. However, the number of receiving labor hours may increase as the number of purchase orders increases. In the short run, even many labor costs may be fixed with respect to the number of purchase orders. If the number of purchase orders is increased by 10 percent, it may not be necessary to hire any additional people for receiving. If there is slack capacity and no alternative use for the labor, the marginal cost may be close to zero. However, if slack capacity is not available, one additional purchase order may require that one additional person be hired.

Purchase Order Cost Versus Line Item Order Cost

Some organizations find it useful to separate the purchase order cost and the cost for an additional line item on the purchase order. Once a purchase order for a particular vendor is created, it may cost very little to add additional items to the order. This becomes particularly useful when joint replenishment logic is being used.

This document does not have separate estimates for the two costs; rather, it helps compute the average cost to order a single item assuming that all items on a purchase order share the cost of the order.

Insensitivity to Errors

The economic order quantity calculation is not particularly sensitive to an error in the estimate of the average order cost. For example, a 10 percent error in this estimate will generally cause only about a 5 percent error in the order quantity.

Level of Detail

Many companies find it sufficient to have a single order cost parameter for every item in the entire inventory. Other companies go to the other extreme and have a different parameter for each and every item based on its vendor and other characteristics. Most companies have a different order cost by class of items where the classes are based on issues such as EDI versus mail, inspection versus no inspection, difficult receiving versus easy receiving, costly shipping versus cheap, etc.

Worksheet

The next section includes a simple worksheet designed to help estimate the cost of ordering an item. The worksheet may need to be modified to fit a particular company's approach to handling purchase orders. The following paragraphs explain some of the details of the worksheet.

1. Create the purchase order. Remember to include only incremental costs here.
2. Communicate the purchase order to the vendor. Usually only one mode is used. If more than one is used, it might be necessary to weight the costs by the probability of using that mode. Average expediting cost should also be included with these.

3. Ship the order. Shipping cost is irrelevant to the cost of placing a purchase order if the shipping cost is based on weight, number of units shipped, volume (cubes), etc. Shipping cost is relevant to purchase order cost if there is a fixed cost for each shipment.

4. Receive the order and move to storage. Again, it is important to remember that the relevant costs here are only those that vary with the number of orders. Costs that vary with the unit volume are not relevant. (These costs should be associated with the product cost rather than with the order cost.)

5. Process the vendor invoice for the purchase order. Be careful not to double count the computer processing costs both here and with the cost of creating the purchase order.

Order Cost Calculation Worksheet

I. Create the purchase order.

  A. Average marginal cost for labor and materials
     required to create a PO. $_____

  B. Cost of physically counting the inventory to be
     sure that an order is necessary. (This is not a
     recommended practice.) $_____

  C. Cost of all accounting and computer transactions
     for a purchase order. $_____

  D. Cost of the labor to approve (authorize) the
     purchase order. $_____

II. Communicate the purchase order to the vendor.

  A. By mail.
    1. Cost for postage. $_____
    2. Cost for express mail service. $_____

  B. By phone.
    1. Labor time. $_____
    2. Long distance phone cost. $_____

  C. By fax.
    1. Labor time. $_____
    2. Long distance phone cost. $_____

  D. By EDI.
    1. Long distance phone cost. $_____
    2. Computer time. $_____

III. Ship the order—cost of shipping. $_____

IV. Receive the order and move to storage.

    A. Labor cost associated with paper work and data
       entry. $_____
    B. Inspection. $_____
    C. Unpacking/repacking. $_____
    D. Movement to storage. $_____

V. Transaction cost to handle the invoice for the
purchase order. $_____

Average cost to place a purchase order: $_____
Average number of items on a purchase order: _____
Average cost to order an item: $_____

APPENDIX 6.7   NEWSBOY PROBLEM FORMULATION AND SOLUTION

When making a decision on the last lot buy (final lot buy) for a part, it is necessary to trade off two costs:

1. The cost of having too much inventory, and, therefore, having to scrap some parts.
2. The cost of having too little inventory, and, therefore, having to repurchase (or rebuild) additional parts.

In the simplest form, this problem is called the "newsboy" problem and can be formulated and solved mathematically as follows:

c_o = Unit "overage" cost. This is the cost of having to scrap one unit at the end of the product life cycle. This should be adjusted for the time value of money. This cost is equivalent to the acquisition (purchase) cost less the salvage value plus the carrying cost through the termination date.

c_u = Unit "underage" cost. This is the cost of having one unit less than needed. In a service parts context, this is the lost customer goodwill plus the repurchase cost for the part.

Q = "Optimal" inventory quantity that should be on hand. (Note that the final purchase quantity should be Q less the current on hand and current on order.)

d = Demand per period in units.

$p(d)$ = Probability of a demand of d units over the remaining lifetime of the product. A discrete probability mass function (such as the poisson distribution) was used here. It is also possible to use a continuous distribution such as the normal distribution.

Since c_o and c_u are both cost parameters, taxes should either be considered for both parameters or for neither parameter.

The equation for the expected (average) cost is therefore:

$$TC(Q) = \sum_{d=0}^{Q-1} c_o(Q - d)p(d) + \sum_{d=Q}^{\infty} c_u(d - Q)p(d)$$

The first summation is the expected overage (scrap) cost, whereas the second term is the expected underage (shortage) cost. Using calculus, we find that the mathematically optimal (lowest total cost) inventory quantity can be found as the smallest value of Q such that the following relationship holds true:

$$\sum_{d=0}^{Q} p(d) > c_u/(c_u + c_o)$$

This value of Q can be found with a simple trial and error approach starting with $Q = 0$ and increasing Q until the above relationship is satisfied. Note that when $c_o = c_u$, the right side is .5. This is consistent with intuition that suggests that the optimal inventory will be in the "middle" of the distribution when the costs are equal.

For example, an inventory analyst is faced with a decision to make the last purchase for an item which currently has an inventory of 3 units. The forecast for the remaining lifetime demand is 9 units and it is believed that the demand over the lifetime is a poisson distributed random variable. (The poisson distribution is usually a good assumption for demand that has a fairly low mean.) The forecast is treated as the mean or expected value for the distribution. The parameters c_o and c_u are estimated to be $100 and $1,000 per unit, respectively. (In other words, the cost of stocking out one unit is 10 times that of having to scrap a unit.) The c_u parameter is large because the part will be very difficult to manufacture in the future. The value of Q should then be selected to satisfy the above equation with

$$c_u/(c_u + c_o) = 1{,}000/1{,}100 = .91$$

Referring to a table of poisson probabilities, the following are the probabilities for x given that the mean demand (λ) is 9 units:

Q	$\sum\limits_{x=0}^{Q} p(x)$
0	0.000
1	0.001
2	0.006
3	0.021
4	0.055
5	0.116
6	0.207
7	0.324
8	0.456
9	0.587
10	0.706
11	0.803
12	0.876
13	0.926 <——
14	0.959

The best value of Q can now be found from a simple search to find the smallest value of Q that satisfies the above equation. This value is $Q = 13$. Given that 3 units are already in stock, the final purchase should be about 10 units. If the optimal value of Q was less than 3 (the current inventory position), it might be advisable to scrap some units now.

CASE STUDY

3M Service Parts and Logistics Center

COMPANY BACKGROUND

Minnesota Mining and Manufacturing, better known as 3M, is a $13 billion dollar company headquartered in St. Paul, Minnesota. 3M is a global leader in industrial, commercial, health care, and consumer markets, and is known for its steady stream of innovative products. The company is involved in the manufacturing and distribution of a broad variety of products such as adhesives, video tapes, Post-it℠ notes, microfiche reader/printers, and heart-lung machines. The company has long been noted for its high quality products and innovative corporate culture.

The 3M Hardgoods and Electronics Support Division (HESD) provides services for a wide variety of products manufactured and/or distributed by other 3M divisions. Typical equipment includes microfiche cameras, readers, and printers, safety and security systems found in libraries and in retail stores, engineering drawing storage and retrieval systems, medical imaging systems, and printing and publishing equipment. HESD employs about 550 service technicians in the United States.

HESD SERVICE PARTS AND LOGISTICS CENTER

HESD's Service Parts and Logistics Center (SP&LC) in St. Paul, Minnesota, is the only warehouse for all of HESD in the United States. HESD also supports a service parts center in Europe.

The fact that Xerox, DuPont, Black & Decker, NCR, Ecolab, and other leading companies have benchmarked 3M's service parts operations suggests that 3M has a well-managed service parts organization.

The SP&LC inventory system has about 68,000 part records and stocks about 27,000 parts. Total inventory investment is about $14 million. SP&LC supports a wide variety of customers including:

- HESD service technicians.
- Dealers.
- Original equipment manufacturers (OEMs).
- Retailers.
- Distributors.
- Value added resellers.
- Private labelers.

In the United States, over half of the service parts business is through 3M technicians in the field.

Parts distribution is the primary service offered by the 3M SP&LC. SP&LC provides three types of customer service arrangements:

1. Routine order service. Available 7 A.M.–5 P.M., Monday–Friday, 1–3-day shipment, single or consolidated shipments.

2. Expedite order service. Available 7 A.M.–5 P.M., Monday–Friday, same day shipment.

3. Emergency order service. Available 24 hours per day, 365 days per year, same day delivery (counter-to-counter) or next day delivery.

SERVICE PARTS AND LOGISTICS CENTER WAREHOUSE LAYOUT

The layout of the SP&LC is designed so that the packing and shipping areas are in the center of the building. Rows of shelves are perpendicular to the packing area. High volume/low cube items are located close to the packing area. Low volume/high cube items are kept further back. The packing and freight processing areas are in the middle of the high velocity storage areas so that travel distances are minimized for picking, packing, and freight processing of orders. The SP&LC has separate receiving and shipping docks.

Materials handling costs in the warehouse can be significant. The SP&LC uses the following principles to guide warehouse design in order to minimize these costs:

1. Keep parts with high usage close to the packing area.

2. Do not keep all high demand parts too close together as this can lead to interference between people trying to get to these parts.

3. Keep low volume/high cube parts on pallets rather than on shelves.

4. Arrange the high velocity shelves perpendicular to the packing area so that stock pickers can quickly access needed parts.

BAR CODING AND PROCESS FLOW

Bar coding helps 3M SP&LC in the entire warehouse process, including:

Receiving.

Quality control/inspection.

Stocking.

Picking.

Packing.

Freight processing.

Return parts/warranty parts/control parts.

Most orders received from non-3M vendors come with a packing list that displays the 3M purchase order and all 3M part numbers on the purchase order number. The part number is used to verify the purchase order number and to print a "load ticket" bar code for each part. All parts received from 3M plants are already properly bar coded, labeled, and packaged according to SP&LC standards.

All parts received from certified vendors are moved directly to shelves without going through the quality control and inspection process. All parts from noncertified vendors must pass a careful quality control inspection process.

Loads are moved on a cart that has a computer screen attached to it. The bar code on each load is scanned and the computer screen displays the shelf location for the part. Most items have a "home" location that is selected based on its size and usage rate.

Once a customer order is entered, it is put into the computer's queue of parts to be picked from the shelves. When a parts picker is about to start another trip, the computer builds a trip list and displays it on the computer screen on the cart. The trip list gives the stock picker a minimum distance route to follow. At each stop along the route, the stock picker scans the part number and the shelf number. The computer then checks that the item being picked matches the item ordered.

The packing and freight processing operation requires only a minute or so for each order. The packing person bar codes the part number and then simply follows the instructions on the computer screen. The computer instructs the packer on how to pack the parts and then prints the address on a sticky label and also prints the stamp for Parcel Post, UPS, Federal Express, or RPS mailing.

Bar coding also helps with parts that are coming back through the SP&LC. Three categories of parts come back to SP&LC. These include:

1. Returned parts. Good parts that a dealer or a technician did not need and are returning to stock.

2. Warranty parts. Parts that failed but are still under warranty by the vendor.

3. Control/repairable parts. Parts that contain hazardous materials, are wanted for technical evaluation, or are repairable.

3M technicians will put a bar-coded returned goods tag on parts that are to be returned. The bar code on this tag is scanned when the parts are received at the SP&LC.

Bar coding contributes to both productivity and quality at the SP&LC warehouse. Order fill accuracy has increased to over 99.9 percent. Inventory accuracy is now over 99.9 percent. Bar coding has also helped improve productivity from about 17.8 line items picked per hour up to 20.6 lines picked per hour. Bar coding has also helped traceability, training, and cycle counting. Gary Busson, the SP&LC warehouse supervisor, says, "Bar coding makes our lives much simpler."

CAR STOCK INVENTORY

At 3M the target inventory assigned to each technician vehicle is called the "custody" inventory. If a technician is trained on a product, the target inventory for a technician is based on the average demand rate, the cost of carrying the inventory, and the cost of a no-parts call. The cost of carrying inventory is based on the opportunity cost of having money tied up in inventory. The cost of a no-parts call is the sum of the labor cost for the technician to return to the customer's site, the additional cost involved in express mailing the part to the technician, the lost goodwill for the customer having to wait for the part, the parts handling cost, and the dispatching cost. All parts are considered independently. Ordering costs are not considered relevant because technicians generally replenish their inventories every time a part is used.

The calculation for determining the target inventory level for a technician is based on the poisson distribution. The poisson distribution is a good way to describe the demand for items that have relatively low average usage rates. The custody inventory for a technician is found by an iterative procedure that continues to increase the target by one until the incremental cost outweighs the incremental benefits. (A similar procedure is explained in the chapter on inventory management.)

The above financial analysis is a starting point for determining custody inventory. Technicians are given some discretion so that they can customize their vehicle inventories to their particular mix of customer requirements.

Performance measurement for the custody inventory is based on two measures:

1. Parts Availability Level (PAL). This is the percentage of service calls that require a part from the technician's inventory and the part is available.

2. First Call Completions (FCC). This is the percentage of service calls that are completed during the first visit. About half of all service calls do not need parts. The primary reason for a service call not being completed the first time is not having the right parts.

At 3M, technicians are responsible for managing their own inventory and this is reflected in their performance appraisal.

DISPOSING OF OBSOLETE INVENTORY

Every service parts organization contends with the problem of determining how much inventory to scrap at any point in time. By the very nature of the service parts business, many items have low demand. Even in the best run service parts inventory, many parts will have to be scrapped.

3M is attacking the problem with a sophisticated program called LIDA (Lifetime Inventory and Demand Analysis). LIDA is a decision support system (DSS) that helps 3M inventory analysts determine how many units (and dollars) of each part should be retained and how many should be scrapped at any point in time.

The DSS makes use of the inventory analysts' experience while still employing a sophisticated set of models for forecasting and inventory planning. Only the major features of the LIDA DSS are presented here. Many man-machine interaction issues, database issues, and management report issues cannot be adequately described in this case study.

In a typical interactive session with the DSS, the following activities occur:

1. The analyst logs on and defines a list of the desired products.

2. The DSS finds all parts in the database that are near the end of their life cycle (demand with a negative slope) and also belong to the analyst-specified set of products.

3. The DSS estimates the lifetime demand (demand from the current date to the termination date) for each part using linear, exponential, and power curve fit models. The model with the best fit (minimum mean^2 error) is selected. All parts have 24 months of available history.

4. The DSS determines the mathematically optimal (minimum total incremental cost) retention stock for each part based upon the cost parameters and the forecast of the cumulative demand through the termination date from the best forecasting model. The forecast includes an estimate of the standard deviation of the forecast error. Termination dates, established by management, are typically from one to five years into the future.

5. The DSS sorts the parts in order of recommended scrap value (highest scrap value first) where scrap value is defined as the number of units scrapped times the book value per unit.

6. The DSS presents descriptive, statistical, and graphical information on each part to the analyst with three types of

screens. The *part identification screen* presents a complete description of the part, demand history, vendor information, cost information, average demands, etc. The *graph screen* presents a graph (with character graphics) of the last 24 months of the demand plus the forecasted demand for each month through the termination data for the part. (Multiple screens are used if necessary.) The *decision screen* gives the analyst an opportunity to select a different forecasting model and/or make the retention stock decision. Figures 1 and 2 illustrate the format of the graph and

FIGURE 1
Example Graph Screen

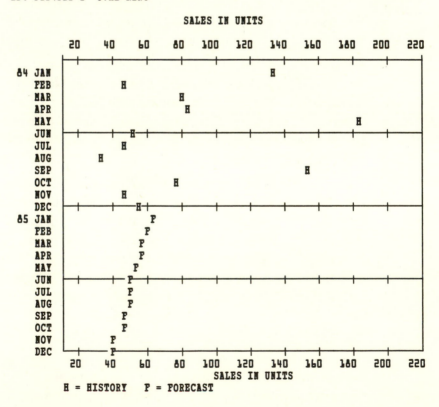

FIGURE 2
Example Decision Screen (Simplified)

```
ID: P234523-1  OVAL RING

RECOMMENDED FORECASTING MODEL:  EXPONENTIAL CURVE FIT
FORECASTING MODEL DECISION:  LINEAR(L)  EXPO(E)  POWER(P)  [E]

CURRENT DATE:       JANUARY 1, 1994
TERMINATION DATE:   JANUARY 1, 1995
NUMBER OF MONTHS UNTIL TERMINATION: 12 MONTHS

                              UNITS           DOLLARS
BOOK VALUE (PER UNIT)                    $     1,000.00
CURRENT INVENTORY POSITION    3,956.     $   395,600.00
EXPECTED LIFE TIME DEMAND       600.     $    60,000.00
RECOMMENDED SAFETY STOCK          6.     $     6,000.00
RECOMMENDED KEEP STOCK          660.     $    66,000.00

KEEP STOCK DECISION:  [       660] UNITS
HIT ENTER TO ACCEPT DEFAULT.  HIT ESCAPE TO DEFER THE DECISION.

  SEE ID SCREEN (I), GRAPH SCREEN (G), OR NEXT PART (N)?  [N]
```

decision screens. (In order to keep the example simple for this case study, Figure 1 has only 12 months in the estimation sample and only 12 months until the termination date.) The default decisions are in square brackets. The analyst can easily switch between the part identification, graph, and decision screens to facilitate the decision process.

7. The analyst can then accept the recommended retention stock, override the recommended value with another value, or decide to defer the decision on this part.

8. If the analyst makes a decision on the retention quantity, a transaction is added to a file that is used to create the paperwork for stock pickers to find and scrap the parts, for the accounting system to record the transactions, and for service engineering to have a chance to review the decision. The next part in the ranked list is then presented to the analyst.

The DSS also produces several useful summary reports to help management ascertain if certain aggregate inventory reduction objectives are being met. These reports include a comparison of the value of the total inventory that the DSS recommended be scrapped and the value of the total inventory that the analysts actually decided to scrap. Most of the reports are by product classification.

The analysts, with the help of the DSS, have been able to maintain low levels of obsolete inventory. The model has been very satisfactory and continues to be used on a regular basis. The analysts believe that the DSS is working well and have achieved significant inventory reductions without having to repurchase significant amounts of inventory.

LIDA has been a success. However, LIDA only attacks the result of the problem (e.g., too much inventory). 3M management is attempting to attack the root problems which involve final buy quantities and forecast accuracy.

WAREHOUSE INVENTORY PERFORMANCE MEASUREMENT

Some of the performance measures currently used by the SP&LC include:

Service Level.   The service level is considered the fill rate which is the percent of orders filled from stock. The SP&LC currently fills about 97.6 percent of all line items from stock. Other service-related variables include the percent of orders that are shipped within the allowable time frame and the age of backorders. The age of backorders is measured as the number of orders that are unfilled for 0–30 days, 31–60 days, 61–90 days, and over 90 days. Significant improvement has been achieved since 3M began paying attention to this measurement.

Accuracy.   Inventory accuracy is the percent of records that have on-hand inventory balances that are within counting tolerance as determined by a semiannual audit. Current inventory accuracy is about 99.9 percent. The bar coding system has made a big impact here. Other accuracy measures include percent of orders received and entered accurately and percent of orders that have the proper item and quantity picked, packed, and shipped.

Quality.   The SP&LC is responsible for the quality of the parts delivered to the end-user. SP&LC currently delivers 96 percent functional on arrival to the customer.

Critical cycle time.   The 3M Corporation is focusing a great deal of attention on cycle times. For the SP&LC, this is defined simply as the inverse of the inventory turnover ratio. The SP&LC is striving to reduce cycle time (increase turnover) by 50 percent between 1985 and 1995. The organization has already achieved some success with respect to this goal. Critical cycle time has been reduced from 19 months (.6 turns/year) in 1985 to about 8 months (1.5 turns/ year) in 1991. Given the nature of 3M's business, this is a dramatic improvement.

CHALLENGES

HESD is considering implementing a new service call management system that has rudimentary service parts inventory management capability. The system has fields for on-order, on-hand good inventory, and on-hand bad inventory in multiple stocking locations. However, the system has no purchasing or warehouse management functionality. SP&LC management is considering how to integrate the existing systems (developed in-house many years ago) with the proposed commercial service call management system. Ideally, this new system will allow the SP&LC to be more flexible and, therefore, more responsive to unique requests from other 3M divisions and from end-users.

KEY POINTS

3M has taken a rather unusual position in the industry in not having any field warehouse inventories. This policy has paid off for 3M.

3M/HESD Service Parts and Logistics Center has shown that information can be used to reduce inventory, improve productivity, and improve customer service. Bar coding, custody planning, and retention stock planning systems are good examples of how 3M has applied this principle to reduce inventory, improve quality, and improve customer satisfaction.

ACKNOWLEDGEMENTS

The author wishes to thank the following 3M people for their help in preparing this case:
Mr. Jim Hall, Process and Industrial Engineering Manager
Mr. Mike Gibson, Materials Control Manager
Mr. Gary Busson, Warehouse Supervisor
Mr. Mike Mazzitello, Inventory Systems Planner

CASE STUDY

Digital Equipment Corporation Digital Services Division

COMPANY BACKGROUND

Digital Equipment Corporation (otherwise known as Digital and as DEC) is a $13 billion company with about 100,000 employees head-quartered in Maynard, Massachusetts. Digital is a leading worldwide supplier of networked computers that offers a full range of desktop, client/server, production, and mainframe systems for multivendor computing environments.

In the 1991 annual report, the president of the company, Mr. Kenneth Olsen, lists four businesses for the company: commodity products (PCs, UNIX workstations, etc.), VAX systems, VAX mainframes, and services. Mr. Olsen elaborates on services with the following comments:

> We offer a wide range of services to do all those things needed to complete the job for the customer. Our service organization designs and installs networks, integrates systems, runs complete information shops,

supports standard PC software, runs networks of PCs, and provides all the services the customer wants, or needs, after our equipment has been shipped. *This business is growing and profitable and is key to our success.* (Italics added for emphasis by the author.)

Field service support plays a significant role in the delivery of these services that Mr. Olsen is referring to here.

DIGITAL SERVICES DIVISION

The Digital Services Division provides much of Digital's services. The management of the Digital Service Division sees the following trends in the marketplace:

- Customers are becoming less and less tolerant of equipment failures.
- Customers are less willing to pay for service agreements.
- The competition among service providers is becoming more intense.
- Service contract prices as a percent of sales price will continue to decline.
- Labor costs will continue to increase.
- The profitability of hardware service businesses will continue to be under pressure.

In light of these factors, Digital's management is attempting to increase the range of value-added products that are offered by Digital's service organizations.

DIGITAL SERVICES LOGISTICS

Digital Services Logistics (DSL) manages hundreds of millions of dollars of service parts inventory worldwide for Digital Services. DSL supports every product sold in Digital's product line.

Digital has about 450 "endpoint" stocking locations worldwide that are supplied from a single national warehouse in Andover, Massachusetts. Rather than have all service engineers (technicians) carry an inventory of expensive boards, Digital's strategy is to have service engineers carry only less expensive parts and have a delivery service pick up expensive boards from local stocking points and bring them to customer sites as necessary.

MATERIALS MANAGEMENT FOR CUSTOMER SERVICE

Effective service logistics management at Digital provides high quality service to customers and a significant financial return to stockholders. Much of DSL's success comes from applying the basic principles of requirements planning and physical distribution. However, management for high-tech electronic equipment is significantly different from most logistics systems because many of the parts can be repaired at a fraction of the cost of a new part. This case study relates DSL's strategic approach to achieve high performance results in this environment. The remainder of the case is divided into four areas:

1. Strategic direction and channels.
2. Product structure and service targets.
3. Field stock management.
4. Central material planning.

STRATEGIC DIRECTION AND CHANNELS

Customer service logistics is different from traditional manufacturing distribution in that parts are exchanged with the customer rather than sold to the customer. The repair of defective parts is much cheaper than manufacturing or buying a new part. Managing this process requires that the distribution network be viewed as a closed-loop system as shown in Exhibit 1.

Material strategy in a closed-loop system starts with the traditional decisions of:

EXHIBIT 1
Closed Loop Repair System

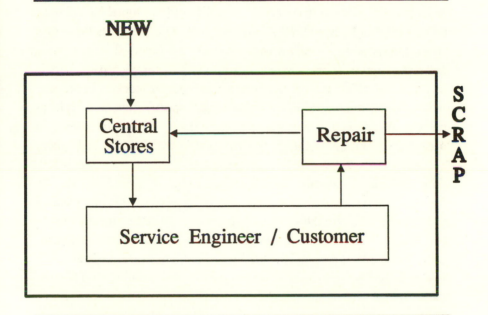

- What to stock.
- How much to stock.
- Where to stock.
- How to deliver.

However, with repairable inventories, DSL's management must ask the following questions:

- How should defective parts be returned?
- Which vendor should repair this item?
- What are the forecasted return rates?

A good decision process in this evnironment can reduce the total cost of materials by 50 percent and have a significant impact on service levels (customer satisfaction) and obsolesence. The materials manager must focus on sourcing parts first through the repair process. The fundamental principle for a closed loop repairable inventory system is, "if you own enough to fill the pipeline, do not buy any more."

DSL's first step in defining a materials strategy is to define a product support plan for each product. In today's service business, these products include many that were not initially sold by Digital but are used by customers who need total service support. This plan lists the FRUs (Field Replaceable Units) for each product, the expected failure rates, and a description of the availability expectations for each part. This is then used to define the echelon where each part is stocked in the network. For example, a terminal product may specify keyboard replacements within 48 hours. This would suggest that keyboards be stocked in a central stockroom location and shipped directly to the site where needed. On the other hand, communication products are essential to most customers' operation. In this case, the strategy would probably be for two-hour response and fix. Parts for this type of product are planned to be stocked close to the service engineer or even at the customer site.

The next step is to define the required logistics network and channels. Based on the cost and availability of rapid delivery, Digital uses a two-echelon network with a central stockroom location and district parts centers. Parts identified for district centers have Target Stock Levels (TSLs) established at every site. (Note: District stocked parts are identified in the product support plan.) Nearly 100 percent of the time, the engineer can obtain a part from local stock. Any part in a product support plan but not stocked locally would be delivered to the engineer the next morning as a priority one order from the central stockroom. The district centers manage the loan of material to the service engineers. The objective is to return parts within 48 hours if not required for a specific service call. Orders for replenishment of TSLs are placed when the service engineer returns a defective part. These orders are automatically generated and networked to the central stockroom for same-day pick/pack/ship. The expectation for replenishment is two days from use to receipt.

Parts that are not listed in a product support plan but needed by a service engineer for a specific situation are ordered on an expedited basis from the product vendor or approved broker. The central stockroom will place the order and provide the service engineer with a committed ship date within 24 hours. If the product support plans are adequate to cover all of the product's functionality, then the parts needed under this mode would be cosmetic panels or unique features.

The delivery channels used by Digital fall into three categories—same day, next day, and second-day deferred. All parts from the district center are delivered to the service engineer on the same day requested. The decision to pick up or deliver is set by a service engineer and his geographic proximity to the supporting disctrict. The central stockroom also offers same-day "next flight out" service for critical customer situations. All priority one orders are shipped from the central stockroom the same day and delivered to the districts by the following day. All replenishment for district TSLs is shipped next day with second-day deferred delivery.

PRODUCT STRUCTURE AND SERVICE TARGETS

The individual product support plans form the architecture by which all service and materials are delivered. It is often possible to define these plans at a product family level rather than for several similar unique products that would have the same service expectations. A hypothetical support plan is shown in Table 1.

To demonstrate the use of this plan, assume that 1,000 units are installed and that they are supported by 50 district sites. The first step is to evaluate the inventory costs of different stocking strategies and the expected level of service. Parts are listed in Table 1 in descending expected failures per year. The total expected consumption is 240 pieces per year (100 + 75 + 50 + 10 + 3 + 2). If we defined a kit of parts as one of each of the six parts and put one kit at every district, we would spend $179,163 for inventory to fill the pipeline. If the low-

TABLE 1
Product Support Plan for Product ABC

Part	Description	Failure per 1000 Installs	Cost New	Cost Repair
29A12335	Color monitor	100	$ 575	$ 205
CB124851	105Mb hard drive	75	320	125
29P45892	Keyboard	50	65	N/A
69329870	3.5 drive	10	175	25
29477883	Power supply	3	803	210
600S5568	Option—full 986	2	1,575	375

est volume part (600S5568) was taken out of the field-stocked kit, over $75,000 would be saved in inventory, and the district service level would be reduced to 99 percent (238 filled/240 consumed). Exhibit 2 shows the graph of level of service versus total inventory as the next lowest volume part is removed from the field kit.

From this data it appears that the best trade-off is to stock the four highest demand parts in the district kit and the last two parts in the central stockroom only. The best approach to this stocking decision is to look at the basic information and then allow the local service manager to input information for specific customer conditions that are different.

Two other pieces of basic information can be collected from the product support plan. First, the total cost of consumption is expected to

EXHIBIT 2
Inventory versus Level of Service

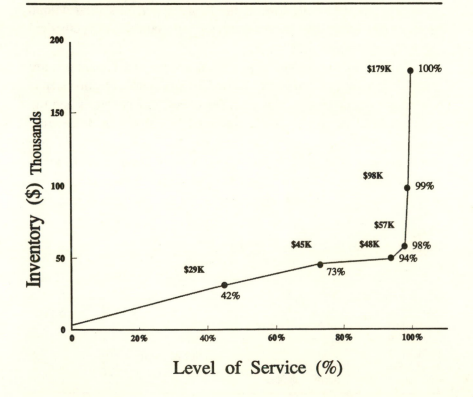

be $92,059 for the 240 pieces consumed. Second, if all the parts are used and repaired with 100 percent yield, the cost of material will be reduced to $34,755, or 38 percent of the total consumed.

With this product support plan in place and communicated throughout the service organization, everyone will have the same definitions and expectations for service levels, inventory investment, and cost of materials. These product plans are also tied through the central planning group, which is responsible for keeping a forecast of trends in the product install base and for maintaining the plans through the various product life cycle phases.

FIELD STOCK MANAGEMENT

Digital's approach to field stock management is to ensure that all material is visible in the inventory system. Exhibit 3 shows how a typical district location would be structured. Each district has a main site with a full-time logistics coordinator (LC), whose responsibility is to control all material within that district and to review and order material as needed to ensure required service levels. All material from the central stockroom will be sent to this location. It is possible, however, to ship to specific customer sites in a priority situation. Each district may have several unique remote or on-customer sites that have material stocked. Parts requested by a service engineer are issued on a "loan" basis and are considered to be an extension of the site stock. When the service engineer uses a part for a customer call, the defective part is returned. A defective material account in each district's main site is used for short-term holding of repairable material. Defective material is sent daily to a central screening area or directly to the repair vendor.

The planning process for material stocked at a district begins with the product support plan. All parts designated as "stock at district" will have a TSL set to 1 in the main site. A TSL operates as a traditional reorder point with one for one replenishment. Digital uses a process that allows the district TSL to be the sum of two factors—kit committed and usage. The kit concept allows the district to establish a collection of parts that are used together. The kit can be a physical kit in a case that the service engineer takes on a service call.

It may also be a logical set of parts that are assigned to a remote

EXHIBIT 3
Local District Material Flow

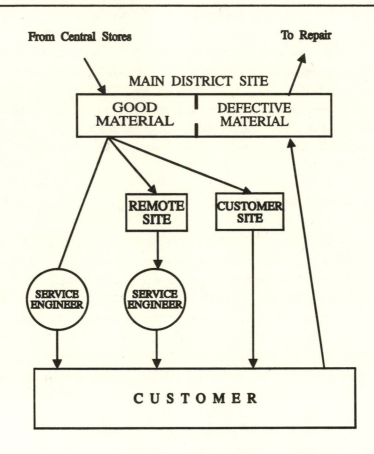

site or a customer site. The kit-committed portion of the TSL is the sum of all kits within the district. The logistics coordinator redistributes material among the various district sites when needed. New material is ordered when the material in the collective sites is less that the TSL. The usage TSL is reviewed regularly to ensure that there is backup stock at the main site or that there is at least one piece of a stocked part in the district.

Every day the system reviews the total district stock against the TSLs and identifies any incremental material orders that need to be placed. These orders are sent electronically to the central stockroom location to be picked/packed/shipped the following day. The logistics coordinator has complete visibility of all orders as they are processed via an order status system. When shipped, the information of weigh bill and carrier is added to the order status. If material is back-ordered, the order status system will appraise the LC with a committed ship date. When a priority one order is placed, it is generally for those parts not stocked anywhere in the district. In this case, the LC can view stock in other regional districts and in the central stockroom and can then decide where to source the parts for the most expedient delivery. The order will ship same day with overnight delivery by 10 A.M. the next morning. Once again, the shipping information is available via order status. This will allow the service engineer to reschedule a service call before the material is received.

CENTRAL MATERIAL PLANNING

The central material planning function has several roles in service materials management.

- Planning for the amount of material required to achieve expected service levels in the central stockroom.
- Sourcing material between repair and new buy to achieve maximum cost savings.
- Maintaining a 12- to 18-month rolling plan for material demand and receipts that can be used for capacity planning and budgeting.
- Expediting nonplanned parts upon request from the field.

The very first step in material planning is to forecast demand on the central stockroom and returns to repair. The forecasting system is based on two years of demand and return history for each individual part. Whenever possible, the forecast for a part is tied to a forecast of the products that use the part. Digital also plans for several other sources of demand for material, including components for the repair operations, outright sale of parts to self-maintenance customers, district initial provisioning for new products, and scheduled material to implement engineering change orders. The key to the accuracy of this forecasting process is to ensure that all possible demands for any given part are included.

The second step in the planning process is to use information on current inventory and purchase orders to develop a plan for future receipts from repair and new buy. This is done by calculating the expected ending stock balance in the central stockroom for each of the next 24 months. When the projected balance falls below a minimum "safety stock" level, the planner schedules new orders as required. Using the material available in repair plus the forecast of field defective returns, the planner determines how much of the total requirements can be sourced from repair. If the expected repair output is less than the total, the planner initiates a purchase order to buy new material for the difference. Generally, the planner places firm orders for material needed within the next 6 months and provides forecasts for the next 12 to 18 months.

The key to making the service material planning process work is to understand that the planner is responsible for ordering material from repair as well as for ordering new parts. If this is not done, the inventory usually grows in the repair centers while shortages exist in the central stockroom. To allow the repair centers to operate efficiently, the central planning group must provide an accurate 12- to 18-month schedule for each part. This allows the repair centers to plan their repair material needs and to adjust their capacity and resources to planned future needs. Planning for external vendors provides information to purchasing and finance with respect to the funds that are required.

KEY POINTS

Digital's management views field service as a key element of their overall corporate strategy. As sales of hardware level off, the corporation sees service as essential to maintaining its customer base and to selling complementary products.

Digital Services Logistics (DSL) supports this customer focus in this service in several important ways. DSL provides excellent availability on the parts and keeps costs low by means of tight inventory control and efficient management of repairable inventories.

ACKNOWLEDGEMENTS

The author thanks Mr. Mark Bittenbender, manager of Logistics Strategic Planning, Digital Equipment Corporation's Digital Services Division, who wrote the first draft of this case study.

CHAPTER 7

SERVICE MANAGEMENT INFORMATION SYSTEMS: MANAGING THE FIELD SERVICE INFORMATION RESOURCE

INTRODUCTION

In the 70s and 80s, manufacturing in the United States and Western Europe was revolutionized by the widespread application of computer-based planning and control systems such as Materials Requirements Planning (MRP) systems. In the 80s and early 90s, field service has undergone a similar revolution with the application of Service Management Information Systems (SMISs), also known as Service Management Systems (SMSs). These systems can support a wide variety of field service activities such as service call entry, dispatching, scheduling, service parts logistics, contracts, technical assistance centers, help desks, sales, accounting, profitability analysis, performance measurement, etc. These integrated systems are built on a relational database so that data is stored in only one place. These systems integrate many different parts of the field service organization with each other—and with other parts of the overall organization. For example, a good SMIS provides for a single contract database that can support both sales representatives and dispatchers.

Most SMISs are built on a fourth-generation database management language (4GL) so that users can add standard reports, perform ad hoc inquiries ("What was our average response time on model Z during June?"), and so on. A good SMIS will have 80 percent of the functionality that a typical field service organization requires; however, some modification is often necessary to fit particular industry-specific and company-specific practices.

145

BENEFITS OF AN SMIS

An integrated SMIS generally has many advantages over internally developed software for a field service management organization. These include:

- Integration advantages. Internally developed software tends to be developed in a piece-meal way and therefore tends to be poorly integrated.

- Business objective advantages. The selling points to senior management include improved labor productivity (for dispatchers, technicians, and warehouse personnel), asset management, customer relations, service quality, market share, and profitability.

- Service call management advantages. An SMIS can support efficient call entry, dispatching, and call escalation so that the response time gap between what the customer expects and what is delivered is minimized. Most SMIS users find that an integrated SMIS can support much tighter management control for both labor and parts. These systems can handle both emergency maintenance and planned service activities such as preventive maintenance and installations.

- Inventory management advantages. An SMIS tracks good and bad parts in multiple stocking locations. Some systems also handle depot repair.

- Customer information management advantages. With an SMIS, the service organization can keep accurate track of the equipment installation, configuration, and repair history for each customer and at each customer site. This can help facilitate quick repairs and can be used as a sales tool for selling service agreements and/or new equipment.

- Contract administration advantages. Nearly all good SMISs have the capability to provide integrated contract information that can support both billing and sales efforts.

- Technical Assistance Center advantages. Many SMISs include (or at least support) expert system applications that can be used to assist technicians and others working in a help-desk environment.

- Cost-tracking/performance measurement advantages. An SMIS will help capture and report data related to labor and parts which facilitates profitability analysis, performance measurement, and billing.

SPECIAL REQUIREMENTS OF AN SMIS

An SMIS is similar to a manufacturing management information system in that it involves large databases, user interfaces, hardware and software, data entry, application development, and so forth. However, the SMIS has several special requirements that are not found in manufacturing. These include:

- Remote data entry from the field. Technicians (and sometimes even customers) enter data from remote locations such as customer sites. Typical transactions include orders for parts and technicians closing a service call.
- Data communications. Data communications are often used to support the remote data entry from the field.
- High-volume voice communications requirements. This is particularly true for service organizations with centralized dispatching and/or a centralized customer assistance center. Voice communications are often managed separately from the information systems function.
- Artificial intelligence applications. The field service organization must often rely on the information system organization for AI expertise in order to develop systems to assist customers in remote diagnosis.
- Contract management. Ideally, contract information should be maintained online and up to date so that the system can determine if a customer request is covered by a service agreement or warranty. The field service information systems must support this critical and difficult application.
- Dispatching and scheduling. Technician dispatching and scheduling is a very complex application involving many difficult

tradeoffs between travel times, training, parts, customer requirements, etc.

- Service parts inventory management. Service parts inventory management is quite different from distribution or manufacturing inventory management. Service parts inventory managers must contend with many slow-moving parts, warranty returns, repairable parts, and multiple stocking locations for each part.

These special requirements make an SMIS particularly difficult to design and to implement. The next section overviews the major modules that are typically found in an SMIS.

SMIS MODULES

All SMISs consist of many modules which can be matched to fit the user's needs. Each module consists of many menus, screens, and reports. Although all commercial SMISs are organized differently, a typical SMIS will have the following modules and/or functions:

- Dispatching/Service Call Management Module. This module supports service call data entry, contract verification, technician assignment, and call escalation. This is generally the central module of the SMIS. This module (or a related module) will support scheduled (planned) activities such as installations, deinstallations, relocations, preventive maintenance, routine inspections, upgrades, or scheduled sales calls.
- Inventory/Logistics Module. This module supports the control and tracking of parts required by customers and technicians. The SMIS will track issues, receipts, and balances at multiple sites and in different conditions (e.g., good versus bad parts) moving through the logistics system. Some SMISs offer purchasing and customer order entry capability. Few of these systems provide complete inventory management features such as stock picking, forecasting, bar coding, or lot sizing.

- Contract Administration Module. Maintaining service contract and warranty information is essential for both billing and sales. Service contracts are extremely complex because customers may have many sites, which may have many systems, which may have many modules, which may have many components. Contracts may cover a site, a group of systems, the customer, and so forth. Unfortunately, the contract logic is not a simple hierarchical ownership relationship.

- Remote Communications Module. Some SMISs have the capability to send and/or receive messages via pagers, hand-held devices, or portable computers. The more sophisticated systems allow technicians to access their service calls, commit themselves to a call, report arrival, receive messages, close a call, and go on to the next customer without having to phone into the office.

- Billing/Invoicing Module. This module tracks labor and parts costs that are to be billed to customers.

- Technical Assistance Center Module. This module supports TAC technicians in call-tracking and handling. A repair history is maintained and is displayed online when needed. The SMIS will capture historical information and use it to help diagnose and solve equipment problems. One of the main goals here is to get the customer back into service without having to send a technician on an emergency service call. Service calls often have to be transferred back and forth between the dispatchers and TAC technicians.

- Repair Center/Depot Module. This module tracks and controls all aspects of the repair depot including parts, work orders, inventory, and billing.

Some SMISs also include the accounting modules (general ledger, accounts receivable, accounts payable, and payroll). However, most field service organizations already have these modules and the SMIS only needs to interface to these accounting systems.

Most SMISs have at least one module not listed above. Some of these include: job costing, forecasting, renting/leasing, and sales support.

A good SMIS will also support some sort of message system. Given the frantic nature of a field service business, it is very useful for technicians, dispatchers, and supervisors to be able to send and receive messages.

INTERFACE TO NEW TECHNOLOGIES

Some SMISs can interface with newer technologies such as:

1. Expert systems for help-desk activities. These issues are discussed in greater detail in the chapter on new technologies.
2. Pagers for communicating to the field. Although pagers are not a new technology, some field service organizations are using paging technology in new and innovative ways. For example, many SMISs will automatically page the technician as soon as a service call has been entered for that technician.
3. Geographical databases for dispatching and tracking of technicians. The concept here is that the dispatcher can have a graphical computer screen that displays the location of all technicians. The dispatcher uses this information in making dispatching decisions.
4. Bar-code reading and printing. Use of bar-coded service parts improves accuracy and efficiency by eliminating manual key entry of data.

CHALLENGES

Implementation of an SMIS is a nontrivial process. These systems invariably change the way that the field service management organization does business. At least three types of changes need to occur when a service organization converts from a manual/internally developed system to an integrated SMIS. These changes include:

1. Customer interface.

2. Decision processes.

3. Terminology.

At the highest level, the field service organization might change the way that it deals with its customers. More information is generally available and the SMIS can often provide much greater decision support capabilities. However, the additional information and capabilities might lead to different policies regarding the customer interface.

Changes may also occur in how decisions are made by dispatchers, supervisors, inventory managers, and others. Many SMISs provide more information for decision making. The information is also provided in a different format.

At the operational level, the SMIS will probably not use the same terminology as the service organization. For example, the SMIS might use the term *technician,* whereas the service organization may have used the term *field engineer* for many years.

Other implementation challenges include the initial population of the databases and developing the disciplines that are necessary to maintain the data. For example, contract data is one of the more difficult databases to encode. Service parts are also difficult, given the complexity associated with serial numbers, revision levels, outgoing parts, return parts, toxic materials, warranty returns, and so on.

CONCLUSIONS

Just as computer-based material requirements systems revolutionized factory materials management in the 70s and 80s, Service Management Information Systems are revolutionizing field service management in the 80s and 90s and beyond. These systems provide an integrated database and complete functionality for a service organization to manage its customers, customer equipment, contracts, technicians, dispatchers, and service parts.

An SMIS serves many purposes. It improves efficiency for dispatchers and technicians, captures service call transaction data, provides exception reports on problem service calls, orders and tracks service parts, provides many management reports, and so on.

The SMIS plays a central role in the integrated organization that has been a theme of this book. The SMIS is a means to achieve integration within the organization. An SMIS should interface with the following systems: accounting (for billing and accounts receivable), engineering (for product design feedback and for repair information), manufacturing (for feedback on conformance quality problems and for service parts planning), human resources (for training information and plans), sales (for sales leads and installation plans), and others.

Integration is essential to the success of a field service organization. Field service organizations often fail the customer simply because they do not have the right information at the right time—which results in not sending the right technician, not having the right part, or not arriving on site at the right time. A Service Management Information System can provide a mechanism for integrating the data and, therefore, provide an integrated customer interface.

ACKNOWLEDGEMENTS

The author wishes to thank the following people and organizations for their help in preparing this chapter:

Mr. Paul Weinberg
The DATA Group
77 South Bedford Street
Burlington, MA 01803

Mr. Larry Miller and Mr. Mike Burns
Service Systems International, Ltd.
8717 West 110th Street, Suite 600
Overland Park, KS 66210

Ms. Ilene DeJong
Applied System Technologies, Inc.
100 Highpoint Drive
Chalfont, PA 18914

CHAPTER 8

INTERFUNCTIONAL CONNECTIONS: MANAGING THE INTEGRATED ORGANIZATION

INTRODUCTION

Field service is closely connected to several other business functions. In order to provide a more integrated view of field service management, this chapter will discuss each of the following interfaces:

- Field service and sales/marketing.
- Field service and design engineering.
- Field service and manufacturing.
- Field service and human resources management.
- Field service and information systems.

The theme of this chapter is that field service cannot be managed effectively in isolation from the other functional units of the organization. Management can often find powerful new approaches to improving customer satisfaction by studying the interfaces (the "white spaces") on the organizational chart.

This chapter will be presented in the context of a manufacturer providing first-party service to its own customers. However, the concepts in this chapter can also be applied to other types of service organizations as well.

FIELD SERVICE AND SALES/MARKETING

Field service involves many interfaces with sales and marketing issues including:

- Marketing strategy.
- Market intelligence.
- Sales.
- Presale and postsale support.
- Service contract design.
- Billing.
- Pricing service agreements.
- Forecasting.
- Product termination policies.

Each of these topics will be discussed below.

Marketing Strategy. As discussed in the chapter on strategy, field service and support can play an important part in a marketing strategy. Field service is an insurance policy for many customers. Good field service can help the company position itself in the high-margin, time-sensitive market niche. Field service also has a major impact on overall customer satisfaction, repeat business, and sales of facilitating products.

Market Intelligence. Technicians are good sources of market intelligence. Technicians spend much of their time working with customers at the customer sites on the customer's problems. They can scan the environment and identify opportunities for new product features, complementary products, and complementary services probably better than anyone else.

Sales. Field service people often have more contact with the customer than anyone else. Customer perception of the quality of the company is strongly influenced by their relationship with the technician. This impacts sales of facilitating products (paper, ink, add-ons, etc.), sales of service agreements, sales of new models, and sales of other products. Service during the warranty period is particularly important to the customer's perception of the value of the service agreement. Some companies use their technicians as salespeople for service agreements and renewals of service agreements. Technicians can also be good sources of sales leads.

Technicians often build a large reservoir of goodwill with their customers. Customers often consult technicians on equipment selection decisions. One technician reports that the level of trust between him and his customer was so high that if he suggested that the customer spread toothpaste on the front of the machine, the customer would do it without asking any questions.

At least one service organization has considered the idea of having technicians call the customer within 60 days of the expiration of the service agreement in order to make sure that the machine is performing well. If the machine has not had any emergency maintenance calls in the last six months or so, it may make sense to perform a PM on the machine just to show some commitment to the customer and to increase the probability that the customer will buy the next service agreement.

Presale and Postsale Support.   Technicians can also play an important role in making a demonstration machine available and/or demonstrating the product. They often install the equipment and train the end-users. These sorts of activities can influence sales by demonstrating the level of service, quality, and commitment that the customer can expect after taking delivery of the equipment.

Service Contract Design.   After the warranty period (free maintenance period) has expired, most service organizations sell service agreements that promise field service coverage over a certain time period at a fixed price. Preventive maintenance coverage is often included in the service agreement. Traditionally, service organizations have offered a standard set of terms and conditions for a specific type of service. The customer either accepted or rejected the service contract that was offered. The trend is towards customizing the service agreement to better meet the needs of the customer with respect to:

- On-site technicians. Does the customer need technicians on-site?
- Maximum response time. Does the customer need a two-hour maximum response time? Should the contract say two hours "on average"? What should be done if the maximum response time is not met?
- Customer-installed peripherals. Is the customer willing and able to install part of the equipment in order to reduce the price?
- Telephone help desk. Should this be bundled with the service contract or sold separately?
- On-site versus depot repair. Is the customer willing to bring the machine into a depot for repair?

Billing. Technicians often get closely involved in the billing process when they make charge calls where the customer is charged for the time and materials that are consumed in the repair process. The customer is usually charged a flat fee, plus a variable rate based on the technician's time, plus the charge for the parts. These calls are normally priced very high in order to encourage customers to purchase service agreements.

One billing problem that plagues nearly all service organizations is determining if a service request is covered by a service agreement or not. Most organizations struggle with issues such as not having a new service agreement on the computer or a service agreement that has just expired.

Pricing Service Agreements. Determining a price for a service agreement is often a difficult issue. The practice in many industries is to set the service agreement price as a percentage of the original product cost (or lease). Some of the more sophisticated field service organizations have segmented the market so that each market segment has a different bundle of goods and services which are priced accordingly. For example, medical imaging equipment may need to have a guaranteed response time of less than three hours. This premium response time may require a premium price.

Forecasting. It is important for the sales/marketing function to share information with the field service organization so that field service can anticipate and schedule installation, training, and changes in technician workforce levels.

Product Termination Policies.   Many companies allow service parts to stagnate in a warehouse for many years before they are disposed. A much better policy is to determine a termination date for a product and then no longer carry the service parts that are uniquely required to support that product. A product termination date should be based on the following tradeoffs:

- Future sales of parts and services.
- Cost of carrying the parts.
- Desire to give the customer motivation to purchase or lease newer products.

Of course, if a part is used in multiple products, some parts may need to be carried until all products that need that part have been terminated.

FIELD SERVICE AND DESIGN ENGINEERING

Engineers must make difficult life cycle cost tradeoffs during the design phase of a new product. The CIRM book by Steve Rosenthal discusses many of the design issues relevant to field service. The product life cycle has many phases—all of which require interaction between field service and engineering. Each of the phases in the product life cycle will be discussed here.

New Product Identification Phase.   Field service technicians are frequently on the customer's site, provide customer training, and know the customer and the customer's needs better than anyone else. Obviously, field service experience can be a valuable source of market intelligence when identifying opportunities for new products and identifying opportunities for improving existing products.

The Design Phase.   Many service organizations have horror stories to tell about how a poor design inflicted the service organization with a piece of equipment that was nearly impossible to repair. Field service should never be used as a substitute for good product design. It is very clear that good field service cannot completely atone for a short-sighted product design.

Engineers must design new products that meet certain minimum serviceability requirements. The field service organization should participate in the definition of these requirements. When designing a product, design engineers should be very concerned about the mean time between failures (MTBF). (The mean failure rate is the inverse of the MTBF.) The MTBF is a function of the reliability of all of the components in the machine. Engineers should also be very concerned about the mean time to repair (MTTR) and the mean time to diagnose (MTTD). These parameters affect the repair time for technicians in the field and, therefore, impact the life cycle cost of the product. Even when the time value of money over the life of the product is considered, significant life cycle cost savings are often possible by making machines easier to repair.

Machines are made easier to repair by using modular designs and by building in self-diagnostic devises. Modular designs make it possible to repair at the modular level rather than the component level. (Modular design also has advantages for manufacturing as well.) Self-diagnostics can often allow the user to diagnose and sometimes repair a problem without a technician visit. If a technician visit is required, this information can be used to increase the probability that the technician brings the right parts. Self-diagnostic devises are discussed further in the next chapter on advanced technologies.

Engineers must define diagnostic and repair procedures during the design phase of the product's life in order to explicitly make the tradeoffs between initial product cost and longer-term maintenance costs. A significant part of this effort is the verification and testing of specific diagnostic procedures. Many companies have serviceability engineers who perform these tasks.

Pilot and Start-Up Production Phase.   During the beginning of the manufacturing phases of the product life cycle, field service and engineering must develop the technical publications, training manuals, and service documentation that are necessary to support the product.

Ongoing Production Phase.   Engineering and manufacturing need to receive performance feedback information from the field so that the product can be improved over time. A formal system for this effort should help engineering identify the 20 percent of the causes that make up 80 percent of the problems. Service procedures must also be improved and kept current during this period as well.

Postproduction Phase.   Most service organizations continue to support products long after they are no longer manufactured or sold. Product improvement efforts may be diminished or eliminated during this phase.

FIELD SERVICE AND MANUFACTURING

Manufacturing and field service interface in the areas of service parts manufacturing and quality. A forecast of service parts requirements is needed in order to feed the master production schedule for the Materials Requirements Planning system. Service parts demand is independent demand that can be added to the gross requirements in the planning records for the service parts. These forecasts are generally provided by the service parts people. The forecasting method here is often exponential smoothing with trend and seasonal patterns. Service parts planning for initial buys and for final buys is discussed at length in the chapter on service parts management.

Some people have suggested that machine population and aging information should be helpful in making these forecasts. Some have even suggested that service parts demand is dependent demand which can be planned in the same way that production can be planned with MRP. Clearly, machine population and age do affect the demand for service parts. However, few organizations have yet to be able to directly take advantage of this information for planning production.

Lack of conformance quality in manufacturing directly affects the field service organization. The cost of a failure under warranty or a service contract detracts directly from profitability. Defect information should be fed back to the manufacturing organization in order to help prioritize continuous improvement efforts.

The famous Maytag ad with the eternally idle technician hopefully waiting for a service call is not about field service—it is about high-quality product design and high conformance quality that makes field service unnecessary.

FIELD SERVICE AND HUMAN RESOURCES MANAGEMENT

Field service is a labor-intensive service business. Field service is a "factory" where most of the factory workers are located in remote areas away from the management. Technicians are the key element in the success of the operation. Great care must be taken to properly select, train, equip, motivate, manage, and reward technicians. A number of service organizations have found themselves in big trouble by not properly managing their technicians. The CIRM book by Lloyd Baird discusses many issues related to human resources management that are relevant to managing a field service workforce.

Training is one particularly difficult issue for field service management. A question that is often asked is, "Should we train just a few technicians or train all technicians on a particular product?" Some companies have elaborate models and/or simulations that attempt to answer these questions.

Some training can be done on the job with a buddy system. Some training can be done best in a training center with the proper equipment and expert trainers. Videotape training has been found to be of some value in some businesses.

Some organizations have attempted to minimize the need for training by applying artificial intelligence (AI) to develop expert systems. These expert systems can make it possible for a novice to diagnose and repair a machine without detailed training on the particular model. The chapter on advanced technologies suggests that AI systems may enable service organizations to get by with less detailed training. The detailed knowledge resides in the computer that the technician carries or accesses via a modem.

An important element of the training program should be people skills. The section on service recovery in the service call management chapter of this book presents some of these concepts.

Technicians are often the best people to train the customers/users. This is particularly true for more complex equipment. Technicians, therefore, may need to be trained in how to be trainers for the customers.

Computer-based training (CBT) has been a popular subject for many years. However, it has only been in the past few years that sophisticated new courseware authoring tools have made CBT really practical. Some vendors of complex equipment are experimenting with the use of computer-based training programs that they bundle with their hardware. One telephone company, for example, has developed a Macintosh CBT program with the Authorware software. This program teaches how to use the phone by leading the student through all of the phone's functions. As CBT becomes more widely available, technicians only need to provide the CBT software for customers. CBT may also have an impact on technician training as well.

The chapter on performance measures lists many different measures that are being used to evaluate technician performance. This chapter points out that many of these measures have problems and should not be used for incentive systems. The closer the incentives are to the overall organization's bottom line, the less likely the incentives will create problems.

One excellent human resources management idea is to encourage nontechnicians to go on field service calls along with technicians. In this author's opinion, it should be a requirement for all managers in the field service organization to go on at least one service call per year. It would also be very useful for managers in sales, manufacturing, and engineering to also go on a service call on a regular basis. This gives managers a better idea of how customers use (and abuse) equipment and allows them to feel the customer's pain and to experience the customer's grief.

FIELD SERVICE AND INFORMATION SYSTEMS

The Service Management Information Systems (SMIS) chapter describes application software for a field service business. The chapter emphasizes the importance of the SMIS to the integration of field service activities with other business functions such as sales, accounting, and engineering.

Field service is an information-intensive business and therefore must rely heavily on the management information systems (MIS) organization for application software development. The interface between field service and the MIS organization is very important to the success of the field service organization. The field service/MIS interface is similar to the manufacturing/MIS interface in that the field service organization requires large databases, user interfaces, hardware and software, data entry, application development, etc. However, the field service/MIS interface has many special requirements. As noted in the SMIS chapter, these special requirements include:

1. Remote data entry from the field.
2. Data communications.
3. High volume voice communications requirements.
4. Artificial intelligence applications.
5. Contract management.
6. Dispatching and scheduling.
7. Service parts inventory management.

Many information system organizations do not have the internal expertise to handle all of these requirements. Most field service organizations, therefore, have their own internal information systems and communication systems managers who work together with the information systems organization to meet the needs of the field service organization.

CONCLUSIONS

Field service is a unique organization. The interfaces between field service and marketing, sales, engineering, MIS, etc., are also unique. Understanding these interfaces is critical to the success of the field service organization and the entire firm. Managing these interfaces is critical to achieving breakthrough levels of customer satisfaction and profitability.

Field service can play the role of the eyes and ears for marketing intelligence, manufacturing improvement, and engineering design—if the organization recognizes this opportunity and takes advantage of it. With an integrated view, field service is a strategic weapon that can be used for powerful competitive advantage.

CHAPTER 9

ADVANCED TECHNOLOGIES FOR FIELD SERVICE MANAGEMENT: MANAGING TECHNOLOGY FOR COMPETITIVE ADVANTAGE

INTRODUCTION

Many advanced technologies are already impacting methods for diagnostics, communications, and management. Some of the most important new technologies include:

- Artificial intelligence.
- Machine intelligence.
- Predictive maintenance.
- Advanced communications technologies.

Each of these will be discussed briefly below.

ARTIFICIAL INTELLIGENCE

As Jeff Pepper emphasizes in his book, *We're Off to Seize the Wizard: The Revolution in Service Automation* (1991), service is a knowledge-intensive activity. Artificial intelligence (AI) is an approach to decision making that takes advantage of knowledge (decision rules) imbedded in software. AI has been applied in many contexts including medical decision making, geological exploration, and circuit design. According to Pepper, AI has been applied to the following field service problems:

37% Troubleshooting (TAC/hotline).

32% Troubleshooting (Technicians).

10% Troubleshooting (Customer use).

8% Expert dispatch.

8% Planning.

1% Other.

The numbers for each problem type reflect the number of applications that Pepper found in a 1991 survey of 3,500 subscribers to the AFSMI Professional Journal. (It is not clear why the numbers do not add to exactly 100 percent.) Pepper reports that about 22 percent of all service organizations in his sample have undertaken projects to build some sort of intelligent system.

Computer technology is now available for AI systems to run on a microcomputer in the technician's hands and/or on a terminal that communicates with a remote mini or mainframe computer. An AI system for diagnosis and repair can offer the following benefits:

- Provides a well-documented formal approach to machine diagnosis and repair that can be implemented consistently in the field.
- Makes enormous amounts of technical information (including drawings) available where it is needed. The amount of information necessary to support products in the field is increasing rapidly. No technician can know it all, and few technicians have either the room or strength to carry all of the manuals that accompany a typical high-tech product.
- Reduces training costs for technicians because the intelligence is stored in the AI system rather than in the technician. This is a particularly powerful concept for companies that have a high-cost training environment—those involved in third-party service (TPS) for a large number of products, those that have a large number of models, and those that have a rapid rate of new product introduction.
- Reduces mean time to diagnose (MTTD) and mean time to repair (MTTR) because technicians are quickly directed to problems.

- Empowers nontechnicians to help the customer repair their own machines via phone consultation.

Although AI systems have a great deal of potential, AI is not a panacea. Some of the problems include:

- Costly systems development. Experienced expert system developers are sometimes difficult to find. The required skills are quite different from those required for applications software development.
- Hard to find expertise. An expert system must imbed true expertise in the software. The expert system will be no better than the expertise that is imbedded in it.
- Difficult software/database maintenance issues. Many technologies are moving targets. As the hardware and software change, so must the expert systems that are used to support them.
- Difficult implementation issues. Users (and experts) will sometimes resist expert systems because of a perceived threat to their jobs.

MACHINE INTELLIGENCE

Many manufacturers are finding a very attractive return on investment in designing machines that have some "intelligence," which makes it possible to monitor a system, detect problems, automatically report the problem, and, in some cases, facilitate remote repair. (In some situations, these systems are called artificial intelligence systems; however, in many cases these are not true AI systems, but rather more basic types of technologies.) These technologies are already widely used for mainframe computers, telephone switches, and sophisticated copy machines. The book by Henley and Kumamoto (1985) is devoted almost entirely to the subject of system monitoring.

Monitoring systems generally have the following elements:

1. Sensing elements—to monitor the equipment.
2. Logic circuits—to process information collected by the sensing elements.

3. Communication capabilities—to communicate the problem to the operator or the service provider.
4. Countermeasure capabilities—ability to affect change in the equipment (e.g., shut down, change parameters, etc.).

Monitoring systems can be completely resident in the equipment or they can be "inquired" by remote equipment. For example, Honeywell will inquire the status of heating and cooling equipment and will report problems from a central location.

Intelligent machines can offer several advantages including:

- Better timelines. Reduces the delay between the equipment failure and the time that the service organization receives a request for service. The remote information can also be used to predict when a machine will fail (see the section on "predictive maintenance" in this chapter).
- More technical detail. Gives the technician some technical information about the problem that the typical user might not be able to discern visually.
- Remote diagnosis and repair. The technical details sometimes allow technicians or even nontechnical people to diagnose and repair a problem remotely. Remote repair is often possible for software-driven systems.
- Service parts requirements. Good remote diagnosis can provide information that can increase the probability that the technician will bring the correct parts to the service call.

Pepper (1991) provides a good illustration of this type of system in his case study of the NCR "ESPm" expert system that runs on the NCR Tower (I-9000/10000) family of mainframe computers. ESPm was developed by NCR to combat the cost of conventional on-site hardware maintenance and to provide some troubleshooting expertise on the customer's site, 24 hours per day. ESPm has two components—a "health monitor" that runs unattended on the customer site and an expert system that resides in NCR support centers and interprets error logs sent to it by the health monitor. The health monitor watches for error conditions such as repeated memory errors or faulty disk sectors.

The expert system consists of several hundred rules obtained through extensive interviews with NCR specialists including remote support field service technicians. NCR reports that the advantage of this system is that it helps predict problems before they occur and allows NCR to schedule technicians in a proactive, rather than a reactive, mode.

Pepper also reports a similar success story with the IBM 3890 check sorter. Stiff competition from third-party services had captured almost 40 percent of the check sorter service business. IBM developed an intelligent system that runs on a PC and sifts through error codes and decides what action, if any, needs to be taken. If the problem is serious enough to require an on-site service call, the system can take the malfunctioning unit offline, log a service call to the IBM service center, formulate an action plan for the service, and even suggest what parts the technician should bring. The system's diagnostic accuracy is 90–95 percent, far better than the performance of the average technician. The result for IBM has been that they have won back every single customer to their service. Overall technician labor hours have been reduced by 22 percent as a direct result of the expert system, and IBM has been able to reduce its service charges. With the ability to use the expert system to reduce downtime and to reduce maintenance costs, it has become an excellent marketing tool.

Machine intelligence is clearly an important technology for the future. However, for smaller, less expensive machines, it is unlikely that this technology will make a difference in the foreseeable future.

PREDICTIVE MAINTENANCE

As illustrated by the NCR and IBM systems, an important application of machine intelligence is in the area of what is called "predictive maintenance." The concept of predictive maintenance is simple: Predict when it will break and fix it just before it does. This is an improvement over the long-discredited concept of, if it isn't broke, don't fix it.

In contrast to predictive maintenance, the typical emergency maintenance or remedial maintenance concept is, fix it when it breaks, and the normal preventive maintenance approach is, fix it at regular intervals so that it will not break. Whereas typical preventive maintenance schedules service calls at regular time intervals, predictive maintenance schedules a preventive maintenance service call based on process control information from the machine.

Cox (1991) relates a story about how sailors in the early 1950s would place one end of a screwdriver against the bearing housing and the other end against their ear to listen to propeller shaft noise. A low-frequency rumble meant that the bearing was fine, whereas a high-frequency screech meant that the bearing would soon fail.

A similar example is checking for turbine cracks in power generation equipment. The cost of predictive maintenance to detect and repair cracks in turbines is about $100,000 over the life of the turbine. However, if a turbine breaks, the results are disastrous—an average repair takes 984 hours and costs about $6 million. These stories illustrate how important it is to attempt to anticipate failures before they occur.

Predictive maintenance requires the use of tools such as monitors and signature analysis to collect data from the equipment. For example, for motors and generators, data is collected on variables such as heat, noise, vibration, and horsepower. This data can then be analyzed using simple trend analysis and/or statistical process control concepts in order to determine the proper timing for a preventive maintenance service call.

The potential advantages of predictive maintenance over emergency maintenance and over scheduled preventive maintenance include:

- Increase the mean time between emergency service calls (decrease the number of emergency maintenance service calls that are required).
- Decrease unneeded preventive maintenance service calls.
- Reduce parts inventories (due to fewer major failures).
- Decrease time to repair.
- Increase system uptime (availability).
- Reduce total maintenance costs for the service provider.
- Reduce cost of ownership for the customer.
- Increase competitiveness for the service provider.

Historically, predictive maintenance has been particularly important for heavy equipment when the repair cost is far in excess of the cost of testing equipment. However, as noted previously, the trend is toward building more intelligent equipment that can support the concept of predictive maintenance. The above list of advantages suggests that the trend toward predictive maintenance may lead to more of a win-win situation for both service organizations and the customers.

ADVANCED COMMUNICATIONS TECHNOLOGIES

In essence, managing a field service organization is like managing a factory where most of the factory workers are working in other people's buildings, traveling, or sitting drinking coffee in a restaurant waiting for the next customer order (service call). A good communications system is essential to success in this environment. This section will briefly discuss some of the communications technologies that form the foundation of any communications system for supporting field service management. Specifically, this section will overview the following issues:

Automatic call distribution systems (ACD).

Paging systems.

Cellular phones.

Radio frequency communications.

Locator systems.

Satellite communications.

The intention is not to evaluate the economics of the technologies or the detailed technological specifications—these are changing too rapidly to be evaluated here. Rather, the intention is to overview the management implications of the technologies so that aspiring field service managers and other managers can have a more thorough understanding of the relevant tradeoffs related to adapting these technologies.

Automatic Call Distribution Systems (ACD)
These are basically just sophisticated phone systems that use computers to direct calls. These systems can perform tasks such as routing a phone

call to a particular phone. If the phone is not answered within a management specified number of rings (or minutes), then the call is redirected to another group. The ACD system captures and reports a wide variety of useful statistics such as:

Average call hold time.

Average talk time.

Number of callers that abandoned a phone call.

Average time available for people taking phone calls.

Distributions for most of the above variables are also collected so that management can "manage the tail" of the distribution. Very often averages (or even medians) are not very useful. Management needs to know what percent of the service calls take longer than X minutes (say, 10 minutes). Simply knowing the average hold time is not enough. A good way of managing call hold times with ACD phone statistics is to set a policy such as "90 percent of incoming calls should have a hold time of less than X minutes."

Many managers also attempt to manage talk time. As noted in the NCS case, there is some debate over this issue. Certainly short talk time does increase the mean service rate and, therefore, reduces hold time. However, it is not a good policy to try to rush customers or technicians when important information needs to be collected. Measuring and encouraging people to manage hold time should suffice in this area.

Many ACD systems also have voice boxes that allow people to leave a message for one or more people. These voice boxes add excellent value to a service organization because people no longer have to play telephone tag. In other words, information can be communicated efficiently with only one of the two parties actually on the phone. In a sense, these systems buffer the people and create an inventory of information between them so that they can both be more efficient.

Paging Systems
Pagers have been around for many years, but the technology has improved in price, range, and quality in the past few years. The basic concept is very simple: A person dials a phone number (typically toll-free), and the page is sent out via radio frequency networks or satellites

to the pager, which might be carried by a technician or a service manager in the field. The basic advantage of the concept is that dispatchers do not have to wait for a technician to call in order to notify them that a service request requires some attention.

The pager can notify the technician with either a tone or a silent vibration. The simplest pagers do nothing more than notify the user that they should call "home." More sophisticated pagers can communicate codes and even voice messages. Codes often indicate the priority of the message so that the technician knows how quickly a response is needed.

Satellite pages potentially have broader coverage and can penetrate concrete and steel buildings.

Cellular Phones

Cellular phone technology is becoming very popular and has decreased in price in recent years. The advantages are that the technician can easily call the customer and/or the dispatcher. Technicians without cellular phones waste considerable amount of time looking for operational pay phones near the highway. The time wasted per phone call is on the order of 30 minutes per call. Many managers underestimate the tremendous value of managing customer expectations—and cellular phones can be a big help to a technician who needs to call a customer to manage some expectations.

The downside for cellular phones is the cost of the air time. (The equipment cost is very small in relation to the monthly cost of the usage time.) It is particularly difficult when personal phone calls are involved. It is important to have some sort of accountability here.

Radio Frequency Communications

IBM and other very large field service organizations have developed radio frequency (RF) terminals. IBM and Motorola call their device the "brick." These devices provide for portable data entry and data communication. Technicians can receive new service calls, order parts, and close calls without ever having to make a phone call to a dispatcher. The advantages here are very evident to people who use these devices: reduced phone wait time, readily available access to information, easy method for communicating data, and greatly enhanced management control. The disadvantages include some problems with range and dead spots that make it difficult for communication from certain locations. These devices have a longer range than do cellular phones, but are not designed to be used while moving.

Locator Systems

These systems are available to help keep track of technician (or at least technician vehicle) locations. Knowing the locations for all technicians is of some value for dispatching—especially if dispatching is done from one central national location. On the other hand, the system could be viewed very negatively as "big brother" watching.

Satellite Communications

Quickly becoming technologically feasible, satellite communications enable technicians to communicate directly with a satellite. In its simplest form, satellite communication is only one-way to the satellite and only allows management to know vehicle locations. More sophisticated satellite technology permits two-way communication for both data and voice communications.

CONCLUSIONS

Many new and exciting technologies are becoming available for field service. The field service manager must have a deep understanding of how these technologies can contribute to field service performance so that they can be carefully evaluated. Clearly, some of these technologies can offer significant competitive advantages; however, caution must be taken to not buy into a quick-fix sales message.

Whirlpool Consumer Assistance Center

COMPANY AND ORGANIZATION BACKGROUND

Whirlpool Corporation is the world's largest manufacturer of home appliances. The company is headquartered in Benton Harbor, Michigan.

The Consumer Assistance Center traces its roots back to 1967 when Whirlpool introduced the "Cool Line" which was the industry's first toll-free consumer assistance phone line. The Cool Line was so successful that a separate center in Benton Harbor, Michigan, was begun with a 24-hour/7-day-per-week line. An additional center in Knoxville, Tennessee, has recently been opened. Both centers have state-of-the-art technologies and are poised to be one of the first customer service organizations to use information for major competitive advantage. Whirlpool has invested over $20 million in the design of these centers.

Whirlpool views these centers as an important part of their service strategy and as aggressively pursuing excellence. The company's promotional videotape proudly proclaims that "The future of consumer service belongs to the Whirlpool Corporation." In the words of Walt Coleman, the vice president in charge of Consumer Services Operations, "We don't want to only be the best in the appliance industry . . . we want to be the best in all industries."

CAC TECHNOLOGY

Whirlpool's two centers are poised to accommodate an anticipated 9 million calls per year by 1995. This tremendous volume of calls cannot be handled with conventional technologies—this would require significantly more consumer assistance representatives (CARs), a very large switchboard, and a very large stack of manuals. The two new centers apply advanced technologies to ensure customer satisfaction. These technologies include:

1. AT&T Definity Communication System. This is state-of-the-art telephone switching equipment. The technology supports simultaneous data and voice communications, automatic number identification (so that the consumer's profile is quickly displayed on the CAR's screen), and efficient voice and data transfer between work stations and between centers. The system that balances the workload between the two centers can reroute calls if a power outage occurs at either center. The CAC allows consumers to ask questions, acquire up-to-date information, and order parts, so that nearly all of their needs are satisfied in one contact with the CAC.

2. Expert systems. Whirlpool is applying expert system technologies in the CAC to help consumer representatives master difficult subjects such as appliance diagnosis and prebuy advice without having to refer to manuals. These systems reduce the amount of phone time and the number of return calls for the consumer by reducing the time required for library searches.

3. Image retrieval systems. This technology provides each consumer assistance representative with almost instant computer access to all of the service and product information that was previously available only through binders, manuals, and microfiche. Over 200,000 pages of documents are already stored in the image retrieval system. The CD-ROM system can display drawings and text on the screen for the CAR to use as they talk with the consumer.

All of these technologies are supported by the latest in computer network technology. The goal of these systems is to provide consumers with faster and more efficient service. These systems work together to assist consumer service representatives in performing different functions including prebuy advice, use and care instructions, and service call management. Each of these functions is discussed briefly below.

PREBUY ADVICE

While most service organizations use only their phone support lines to help consumers with problems, Whirlpool encourages people to call the CAC with questions about products *before* they purchase. Whirlpool views this as an excellent opportunity to educate consumers about the virtues of Whirlpool products with respect to water usage, energy use, pollution, product features, and many other issues.

With the help of expert systems technology, a Whirlpool CAR can become an expert on selling the product. The CAR asks a series of questions in a very professional way to lead the consumer through a decision tree process to determine his or her needs. One of the underlying philosophies here is that consumers will only be happy if they buy the product that fits their true needs. These phone calls are then followed up with literature mailings and referrals to a local dealer.

One difficult issue here is how to handle questions regarding competitors' products. Whirlpool never wants to criticize competitors' products, but people do ask these kinds of questions. The current policy is to not discuss competitors' products.

USE AND CARE

Another interesting feature of the CAC system is the emphasis on use and care advice. Consumers are encouraged to call the CAC for help on using their appliances. This is particularly helpful to many consumers, given the disdain for reading manuals that is prevalent in our society today. Whirlpool can also learn from the kinds of questions and problems that consumers share during these moments of truth.

CALL AVOIDANCE AND SERVICE CALL MANAGEMENT

Consumers do not want to be inconvenienced by a service call. Whirlpool CARs use an expert system for appliance diagnosis to identify a problem. When possible, the Whirlpool CARs help consumers repair their own machines and, therefore, avoid costly and unnecessary service calls. The expert system can be thought of as a series of questions in a decision tree that is used to discover what is wrong with the product. The answer to one question can lead to another question and ultimately to a good idea of the probable cause.

When a service call is necessary, Whirlpool dispatchs a technician. All of the appliance diagnostic information is given to the technician to increase the probability that the technician has the right parts to repair the appliance at the first service call. Technicians using a laptop computer, cellular phone, and portable printer will have the communication support needed to provide excellent service.

In the near future, the CAC systems will schedule service calls, order parts, and handle refunds, exchanges, and so forth. When an on-site visit is required, the system will search for the first available time that a technician can make it to the consumer's ZIP code. The CAR asks questions such as "would Wednesday afternoon be convenient for you?" in order to schedule the service call in a half-day time slot. Slots are loaded to finite capacity based on an estimate of the work required to do each job.

CHALLENGES

The new technology and the challenging business environment require the CAC to have a very heavy commitment to training. Whirlpool has committed to providing over 80 hours of formal training to all CARs.

Having two centers means that it is necessary to balance the load between them. However, management views the value of having the backup systems as worth the cost.

KEY POINTS

Consumers do not often complain to the service provider. The manufacturers that have their ears to the ground are the ones that will be able to continuously improve. And the ones that can continuously improve are the ones that will succeed in the long run. It is clear that Whirlpool is using the CAC to keep its ears to the ground and is moving closer to the consumer for both presale and postsale activities.

With an expected 9 million calls per year by 1995, technology plays a key role in these activities. The key technologies here are communications technologies (telephone switches, both voice and data transmission) and computer technologies (expert systems, CD-ROM graphical databases, and local area networks).

While the CAC may seem to be a "nice-to-have showplace" to some, the Whirlpool CAC is a strategic initiative that will provide significant long-term payoffs. The CAC database is becoming an important corporate resource that feeds continuous improvement efforts for product quality, reliability, and safety. The CAC is an important means of providing accurate and timely postsales support service to consumers—and a means of gathering information from the marketplace.

ACKNOWLEDGEMENTS

The author thanks Mr. Walter J. Coleman, vice president, Consumer Services Operations, Whirlpool Corporation, for his assistance in preparing this case.

REFERENCES

Chapter 1: Introduction to Field Service Management

Berry, Dick. *Managing Service for Results*. Research Triangle Park, N.C.: Instrument Society of America, 1983.

Bleuel, William H., and Joseph D. Patton, Jr. *Service Management—Principles and Practices*. Second Edition. Research Triangle Park, N.C.: Instrument Society of America, 1986.

Fowler, E.M. "Technicians Needed to Service Complex Office, Factory Machines." *Minneapolis Star Tribune*, December 2, 1990, p. 1J.

Chapter 2: Field Service Strategy: Managing the Field Service Business for Competitive Advantage

Ahituv, N., and O. Berman. *Operations Management of Distributed Service Networks—A Practical Quantitative Approach*. New York: Plenum Press, 1988.

Blumberg, Donald F. "Management Systems for Field Service Productivity Improvement." *Omega* 9, 1981, pp. 419–28.

Blumberg, Donald F. "New Strategy Directions of IBM Service: An Assessment and Evaluation." *American Field Service Management International—The Professional Journal* 14, no. 1 (1989), pp. 14–28.

Blumberg, Donald F. "Strategies and Analytical Models for Improving Field Service Force and Logistics Productivity." *American Field Service Management International—The Professional Journal* 16, no. 1 (August 1991), pp. 8–24.

Chase, Richard B., and David A. Garvin. "The Service Factory." *Harvard Business Review* 67, no. 4. (July–August 1989), pp. 61–69.

Firnstahl, Benson P. "My Employees Are My Service Guarantee." *Harvard Business Review* 67, no. 4 (July–August 1989), pp. 28–32.

Hambleton, R.S. "A Manpower Planning Model for Mobile Repairman." *Journal of Operational Research Society* 33, 1982, pp. 621–27.

Hart, Christopher W.L. "The Power of Unconditional Service Guarantees." *Harvard Business Review* 66, no. 4 (July–August 1988), pp. 54–62.

Heloise. "The Biggest Pet Peeve of Them All." *Good Housekeeping*, October 1991, p. 56.

Hill, A.V.; S.T. March; C.J. Nachtsheim; and M.S. Shanker. "An Approximate M/G/s Model for Estimating Expected Travel Time and Response Time for Field Service Repair Systems." *IIE Transactions*, forthcoming.

Service Operations of the 90's. Fort Meyers, Fla.: Coopers & Lybrand and AFSM International, 1991.

Stalk, G., and T.M. Hout. *Competing against Time.* New York: Free Press, 1990.

Trimble, William J., and Robert W. Duncan (Eastman Kodak Company). *Keeping the Customer Satisfied—A Guide to Field Service.* Milwaukee, Wisc.: ASQC Quality Press, 1989.

Chapter 3: Performance Measurement for Field Service: Managing by the Numbers

Kellogg, Deborah L.; Elizabeth L. Rose; and Richard B. Chase. "Service Quality: A Survey of Current Practice." *Proceedings of the National Decision Sciences Conference*, Miami, Fla., 1991, pp. 1657–59.

Parasuraman, A.; Leonard L. Berry; and Valarie A. Zeithaml. "A Conceptual Model of Service Quality and Its Implications for Future Research." *Journal of Marketing* 49, no. 4 (1985), pp. 41–50.

Chapter 4: Service Quality Management: Managing Customer Satisfaction

Bell, Chip R., and Ron E. Zemke. "Service Breakdown—The Road to Recovery." *Management Review*, October 1987, pp. 32–35.

Hart, Christopher W.L.; James L. Heskett, and W. Earl Sasser. "The Profitable Art of Service Recovery." *Harvard Business Review* 68, no. 4 (July–August 1990).

Morton, Ken. "Automating Customer Satisfaction." *MSM—The Magazine of Service Management*, October 1991, pp. 38–45.

Murdick, Robert G.; Barry Render; and Roberta S. Russell. *Service Operations Management.* Boston: Allyn & Bacon, 1990.

Teas, R. Kenneth. "Expectations, Performance Evaluation, and Consumers' Perceptions of Quality." Working paper, Iowa State University, College of Business, October 1991.

Zeithaml, Valarie A.; A. Parasuraman; and Leonard L. Berry. *Delivering Quality Service*. New York: Free Press, 1990.

Zemke, Ron, and Chip Bell. "Service Recovery—Doing It Right the Second Time." *Training*, June 1990.

Chapter 5: Service Call Management: Managing the Customer Interface

Freeman, David B. "From Which Patch Do You Dispatch?" *MSM—The Magazine of Service Management*, October 1991, p. 41.

Hill, A.V. "An Experimental Comparison of Dispatching Rules for Field Service Support." *Decision Sciences* 22, no. 1 (Winter 1992).

MacPherson, Gordon F. "How Staffing Affects ACD Trunking Requirements." *Business Communications Review*, February 1989, pp. 37–39.

Chapter 6: Service Parts Inventory Management: Managing the Inventory Investment

Brown, R.G. *Advanced Service Parts Management*. Norwich, Vt.: Materials Management Systems, Inc., 1982.

Chua, Richard C.; Gary D. Scudder; and Arthur V. Hill. "Batching Policies for a Repair Shop with Limited Spares and Finite Capacity." *European Journal of Operational Research*, forthcoming.

Fowler, E.M. "Technicians Needed to Service Complex Office, Factory Machines." *Minneapolis Star Tribune*, December 2, 1990, p. 1J.

Hill, Arthur V.; Vincent Giard; and Vincent A. Mabert. "A Decision Support System for Determining Optimal Retention Stocks for Service Parts Inventories." *IIE Transactions*, March 1989.

Miller, D.M.; J.M. Mellichamp; and T.A. Henry. "Analysis of Excess Stock in Multiproduct Inventory Systems." *IIE Transactions* 18, 1986, pp. 350–55.

MRO Stores Seminar Proceedings. Falls Church, Va.: APICS, May 1984.

Patton, Joseph D. *Service Parts Management*. Research Triangle Park, N.C.: Instrument Society of America, 1984.

Suzaki, Kiyoshi. *The New Manufacturing Challenge*. New York: Free Press, 1987.

Tersine, R.J., and R.A. Toelle. "Optimal Stock Levels for Excess Inventory Items." *Journal of Operations Management* 4, 1984, pp. 245–58.

Vollmann, T.E.; W.L. Berry; and D.C. Whybark. *Manufacturing Planning and Control Systems*. Second Edition. Homewood, Ill.: Richard D. Irwin, 1988.

Chapter 8: Interfunctional Connections: Managing the Integrated Organization

Baird, Lloyd S. *Managing Human Resources: Integrating People and Business Strategy*. Homewood, Ill.: Business One Irwin, 1992.

Berry, Michael F. "Evaluating Your Options." *MSM—The Magazine of Service Management*, August 1991, pp. 19–23.

Freeman, David. "Tailor-Made Contracts." *MSM—The Magazine of Service Management*, August 1991, pp. 20–21.

Rosenthal, Stephen R. *Effective Product Design and Development: How to Cut Lead Time and Increase Customer Satisfaction*. Homewood, Ill.: Business One Irwin, 1992.

Chapter 9: Advanced Technologies for Field Service Management: Managing Technology for Competitive Advantage

Cox, Robert C. "Predictive Maintenance: HiTech Service Option?" *American Field Service Management International—The Professional Journal* 16, no. 4 (November 1991), pp. 56–57.

Henley, Ernest J., and Hiromitsu Kumamoto. *Designing for Reliability and Safety Control*. Englewood Cliffs, N.J.: Prentice-Hall, 1985.

Mobley, R. Keith. *An Introduction to Predictive Maintenance*. Florence, Ky.: Van Nostrand, 1989.

Pepper, Jeff. *We're Off to Seize the Wizard: The Revolution in Service Automation*. Verona, Pa.: ServiceWare, Inc., 1991.

Whitaker, Jerry C. *Maintaining Electronic Systems*. Boca Raton, Fla.: CRC Press, Inc., 1991.

GLOSSARY

artificial intelligence (AI) Study of how people do things that are considered intelligent, and the discipline of building computer systems to accomplish those things. AI systems typically involve imbedding many "expert" decision rules into software in order to provide expert advice for making difficult decisions.

call avoidance The practice of attempting to help the customer fix a machine without having to send a technician to the customer's site.

call taker Someone who receives service requests from customers. Synonym: Call coordinator. *See also* dispatcher.

consumables Supplies such as fuel, lubricants, solvents, paper, printer ribbons, cleaning materials, wiping rags, and forms that are consumed by the equipment during normal operation or are used by the technician or customer during maintenance procedures.

contract period of maintenance (CPM) The times during the normal work week that are covered by a service agreement. Typical CPMs include "7 by 24" which is seven days per week and 24 hours per day coverage and "5 by 8 7:00" which is five days per week and 8 hours per day coverage beginning at 7:00 A.M. each morning.

customer engineer (CE) *See also* technician.

dead stock Items that have had no demand for some period of time.

dispatch center The location where dispatchers work.

dispatcher A person who (1) receives service call requests from customers (typically over the phone) and/or (2) communicates service call assignments to technicians. *See also* call taker.

downtime The amount of time that the customer's machine is not available for use. Usually, this only includes normal work hours; therefore, it is necessary to know the standard hours of operation in order to compute downtime.

emergency maintenance call A corrective service call that is not planned and requires almost immediate attention from a technician. Sometimes also called "unscheduled maintenance" or "corrective maintenance." *See also* preventive maintenance.

expected time of arrival (ETA) The time that a technician is expected to arrive at a customer's site.

field engineer (FE) *See also* technician.

field service engineer *See also* technician.

first-party service Service provided by the manufacturer or distributor for the equipment. *See also* second-party service, third-party service, fourth-party service.

fourth-party service Service provided to a second- or third-party service organization. For example, a company might provide depot repair for printer heads to a third-party service company. *See also* first-party service, second-party service, third-party service.

hard-down A machine failure that puts a machine completely out of service.

life cycle cost All costs associated with an item over the entire course of its life including research and development, production, operation, maintenance, and termination.

mean time between failures (MTBF) The average (mean) time between machine breakdowns. This can be determined from component reliability data, or can be calculated from historical performance for the model. The latter method is preferred when this type of data is available. This should be determined as the mean time between failures in terms of calendar days. In other words, if a model has a mean time between failures of 30 days, we would expect it to fail, on average, about once per month. *See also* mean time to diagnose, mean time to repair.

mean time to diagnose (MTTD) The average (mean) time to determine the cause for a machine problem. *See also* mean time to repair, mean time between failures.

mean time to repair (MTTR) The average (mean) time to repair a machine includes the time to diagnose and fix the machine but does not include travel time or administrative time on-site. *See also* mean time between failures, mean time to diagnose.

no-parts call An emergency maintenance call that cannot be completed due to the fact that the technician did not have the required part or parts.

predictive maintenance A type of preventive maintenance that uses nondestructive testing such as infrared detectors, spectral oil analysis, vibration evaluation, and ultrasonics to anticipate when and what maintenance is needed to prevent failure.

preventive maintenance   Actions performed in order to attempt to keep a piece of equipment in working condition. A type of service call that can be planned and is often scheduled at regular intervals. *See also* emergency maintenance call, scheduled maintenance.

rebuild   Disassemble, replace marginal-quality parts, and reassemble. May or may not involve final unit testing. Broad wear tolerances are often acceptable. A short warranty is usually offered. *See also* remanufacture.

refurbished parts   Parts that have been repaired.

reliability   The trustworthiness or dependability for equipment. Often measured as the mean time between failures (MTBF). The probability that, when operating under stated environmental conditions, the system will perform its intended function adequately for a specified interval of time. *See also* mean time between failures.

remanufacture   Disassemble, clean, inspect, and reassemble to meet original equipment specifications. Often includes installing engineering changes, full factory testing, and a new factory warranty. *See also* rebuild.

remote diagnostics   Telecommunications technology that allows a technician at a site far from the customer to phone the failed machine via a computer modem and to run some diagnostic checks on the machine.

repairable parts   Parts that can be repaired (refurbished) and returned to inventory.

response time guarantee   A service guarantee that specifies the maximum time delay between the customer's report of a machine failure and the technician's arrival time on-site.

retrofit   Part, assembly, or kit that is used to replace components already installed on the equipment. Performed on a machine to correct a deficiency or improve performance.

scheduled maintenance   Preventive maintenance that is scheduled at regular intervals.

scrap   Inventory to be disposed of or sold for salvage because the residual demand is small.

second-party service   Service provided by the owner or user of a piece of equipment. Also called "self-maintainer." *See also* first-party service, third-party service, fourth-party service.

self-maintainer   An organization that provides maintenance for its own equipment. Also called "second-party service."

service parts   Parts that are used to repair, refurbish, or upgrade equipment. *See also* consumables, repairable parts.

serviceability   The degree of ease with which a machine can be repaired.

short interval call   A return emergency maintenance call required in a short period of time (typically within one to seven days after the original emergency maintenance call).

soft-down   A machine failure that has crippled the machine but still allows the machine to provide limited service.

spare parts   Synonym for service parts. *Service* parts is generally considered a better choice because the word *spare* connotes that the parts are unnecessary.

T&M   Time and material. A T&M call is not covered by a service agreement and, therefore, must be billed to the customer.

technical assistance center (TAC)   A group of technicians that provides phone and/or remote diagnostic support for customers and/or technicians who are out in the field.

technician   A person with technical training to service a machine. Synonym: technician, customer service representative (CSE), field engineer (FE), service technician, tech, tech rep.

third-party service (TPS)   Service provided by an organization that repairs equipment from other manufacturers or distributors. *See also* first-party service, second-party service, fourth-party service.

UPS   Uninterruptable power system. An online UPS is designed to protect the critical parts of a system. A UPS filters out harmful power disturbances and provides battery backup protection. In the event of a total power loss, the UPS signaling features allow users ample time to complete appropriate shutdown procedures.

warranty   Guarantee that a part will perform as specified over the warranty period. The warranty also defines the recourse that will be taken if the part does not satisfy the specifications of the warranty. Parts are typically repaired or replaced at no cost to the customer if the part fails during the warranty period.

INDEX

About APICS

APICS, the educational society for resource management, offers the resources professionals need to succeed in the manufacturing community. With more than 35 years of experience, 70,000 members, and 260 local chapters, APICS is recognized worldwide for setting the standards for professional education. The society offers a full range of courses, conferences, educational programs, certification processes, and materials developed under the direction of industry experts.

APICS offers everything members need to enhance their careers and increase their professional value. Benefits include:

- Two internationally recognized educational certification processes—Certified in Production and Inventory Management (CPIM) and Certified in Integrated Resource Management (CIRM), which provide immediate recognition in the field and enhance members' work-related knowledge and skills. The CPIM process focuses on depth of knowledge in the core areas of production and inventory management, while the CIRM process supplies a breadth of knowledge in 13 functional areas of the business enterprise.
- The APICS Educational Materials Catalog—a handy collection of courses, proceedings, reprints, training materials, videos, software, and books written by industry experts . . . many of which are available to members at substantial discounts.
- *APICS The Performance Advantage*—a monthly magazine that focuses on improving competitiveness, quality, and productivity.
- Specific industry groups (SIGs)—suborganizations that develop educational programs, offer accompanying materials, and provide valuable networking opportunities.
- A multitude of educational workshops, employment referral, insurance, a retirement plan, and more.

To join APICS, or for complete information on the many benefits and services of APICS membership, **call 1-800-444-2742** or **703-237-8344.** Use extension 297.